HEMI
MUSCLE
70 YEARS

CHRYSLER, DODGE & PLYMOUTH
HIGH PERFORMANCE

HEMI
MUSCLE
70 YEARS

DARWIN HOLMSTROM

CONT

1

Uncorking the Beast

The story of Chrysler's Hemi isn't just legendary; it transcends legend and enters the realm of mythology. And it proves German philosopher Martin Heidegger's theory that the mythological—*mythos*—trumps the logical—*logos*. Even though the logos usually supersedes the mythos in technical application, the human animal, being more comfortable with the familiar and resistant to change, would pick mythos over logos when given the choice. The story of Chrysler's Hemi engine provides a powerful example.

A manufacturer can attain mythic status if it dominates a certain market niche. Any model of Ferrari conjures the image of a mythic sports or grand touring car. Even a manufacturer known for building pedestrian transportation devices can create a legendary model, as Ford did when it created the Mustang. But rarely does a technology become mythological. Perhaps this is because by its very nature, technology is the very face logos presents to the world—and logos is the antithesis of mythos.

OPPOSITE: Since Plymouth snagged the Road Runner and Scooby-Doo wouldn't hit the airwaves until the following year, Dodge had to invent its own cartoon character: the Super Bee.

The new Hemi engine was practically race-ready right off the showroom floor and made Chrysler products competitive in all forms of auto racing.

Yet technological mythos trumping logos is exactly what happened with Chrysler's Hemi engine. The company adopted hemispherical-head technology in an attempt to build an efficient V-8 engine that could compete with the overhead-valve V-8s being produced by Oldsmobile and Cadillac. The unintended byproduct of this effort was one of the most dominant engine designs ever unleashed on an unsuspecting public.

The Hemi, which is simply a dome-shaped combustion chamber, hardly seems like the stuff of myth. The clever design has inherent advantages. A dome-shaped combustion chamber with a centrally located spark plug allows the fuel charge to burn evenly. The flame starts at the center of the combustion chamber and pushes down on the piston with even pressure. It also allows for the use of two very large valves, which is an inherent part of the Hemi design. Technically, when a dome-shaped combustion chamber uses three or more valves, it is called a "pent-roof" design.

The hemi design also brings certain disadvantages. For example, a dome-shaped combustion chamber splays the intake and exhaust valves out at a less-than-ideal angle—Chrysler's original Hemi had a valve angle of 58.5 degrees. This necessitated the use of wide, heavy heads topped by complicated and heavy rocker arms that limited ultimate engine rpm. Thus, hemispherical heads work best on large, torque-laden, low-revving engines that don't rely on ultra-high-rpm power and aren't penalized as much as smaller engines for excessive weight.

This made the hemi an ideal design for the big pushrod V-8s powering American performance cars, engines that emphasize low-end torque over peak horsepower output. But the hemi is not unique to American muscle. In fact, US manufacturers were among the last to take advantage of the design. Since the earliest years of the twentieth century, European automobiles with domed combustion chambers had been winning races around the world. Peugeot began using race engines with pent-roof combustion chambers in 1912. Jaguar and BMW produced passenger cars with hemispherical combustion chambers before Chrysler introduced its first Hemi-powered production car.

Chrysler wasn't even the first US automaker to produce engines with domed combustion chambers. Companies such as Duesenberg and Stutz had produced such cars long before Chrysler began developing its production Hemi. The Welch Tourist, first shown at the Chicago Automobile Salon in 1903, featured a 20-horsepower, two-cylinder engine with hemispherical combustion chambers. This car, built by the Chelsea Manufacturing Company, a bicycle-manufacturing operation run by the Welch brothers in Chelsea, Michigan, is likely the earliest production car to use a hemi engine, beating Chrysler to the market by nearly half a century.

No one doubts that the hemispherical combustion chamber is an excellent design, but that still doesn't explain how this version transcended mere technology and became enshrined in the pantheon of technological godhood. The company certainly did not set out to create an automotive icon with its Hemi. In fact, while the engine was in production, Chrysler never referred to its original domed-combustion-chamber engine as a "hemi." Internally, Chrysler

Howard "Tommy" Thompson driving the wheels off his Hemi-powered Chrysler at Daytona Beach in 1952.

ABOVE: The C-4R was the second Hemi-powered racecar that Briggs Cunningham built for competing at the 24 Hours of Le Mans race.

RIGHT: Cunningham drove this C-4R himself for 20 of the 24 hours of the 1952 Le Mans race because he was nursing a failing clutch and didn't want his aggressive co-driver Bill Spear to destroy it completely.

called it "the double-rocker engine," referring to its complex valvetrain mechanism, and gave it the marketing name "FirePower." The firm would not officially give the engine the proper name "Hemi" until the advent of the second-generation engines in the early 1960s. Eventually Chrysler would go on to trademark the term, spelling it with a capital H from that point on. (For the sake of clarity, we're using the capital H whenever we use "Hemi" as a proper noun for a Chrysler engine in this book.)

BATTLE PROVEN

Racing played an enormous part in elevating the Hemi to mythic status. Hemi-powered cars began winning races almost as soon as buyers could get them out on the dirt tracks found in nearly every county fairground in America. It was on a Detroit, Michigan, fairground track on August 12, 1951, that Howard W. "Tommy" Thompson took the first of what would become many NASCAR checkered flags earned by Hemi-powered cars. In the years that followed, sports-car builder Briggs Cunningham turned in impressive performances at Le Mans with his Hemi-powered specials, and Lee Petty won NASCAR's Grand National championship in 1954 in a Hemi-powered Chrysler. Not long after that, Don Garlits bought a Hemi from a junkyard, installed it in his dragster, and made the engine the dominant force in American drag racing.

Racing would go on to serve an even larger role in the legend of the Hemi during the design's second incarnation in the 1960s, but the rise of the technology to mythological status involved a lot more than just success in competition. After all, Hudson's Hornet dominated NASCAR racing in the early part of the 1950s, yet no one ever considered its side-valve inline six mythological. Clearly, there's more to the ascendance of the Hemi than simple "Win on Sunday, sell on Monday" marketing hype.

Part of the engine's appeal had to do with the era in which it existed. Throughout the 1950s, Chrysler's Hemi V-8 engines consistently produced more power than anything offered by the competition. Anyone marketing the baddest cars built in the United States was certain to make a powerful impression on the brains of 70 million baby boomers as they entered puberty. This was the generation obsessed with cars like no other generation before or since. In his book *Lake Wobegon Days*, author Garrison Keillor wrote that the Lutherans in his hometown drove Fords because the Ford dealer was Lutheran, and the Catholics drove Chevrolets because the Chevrolet dealer was Catholic. Or perhaps it was vice versa. Either way, it didn't really matter; if you were a Mopar guy and you lusted after those Hemi-powered bad boys, you were going to hell either way.

BELOW: Norman "Mr. Norm" Kraus's Grand Spaulding Dodge in Chicago, Illinois, gained a reputation as *the* shop for having a street Hemi properly tuned.

BOTTOM: Don Garlits unloads his Wynn's Jammer dragster at the Lebanon Valley Dragway in West Lebanon, New York, in 1965.

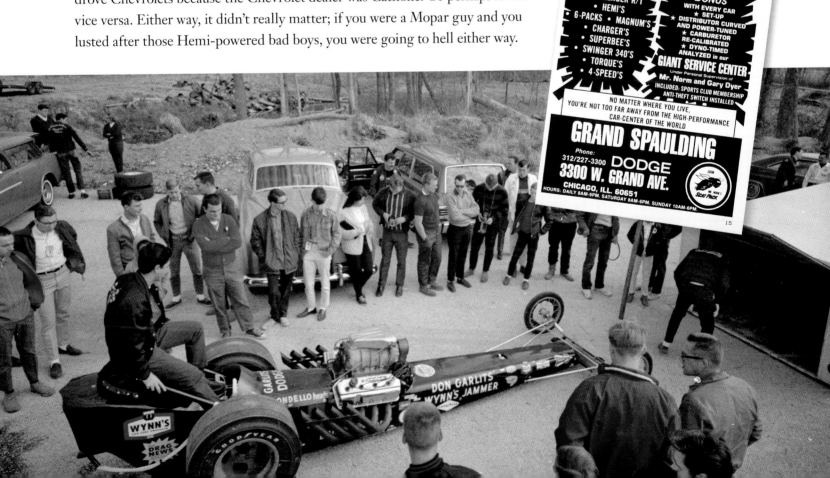

15

World War II spurred massive advances in engine technology. Chrysler used hemispherical combustion chambers in the V-16 engine it developed for the P-47 Thunderbolt.

As has always been the case, young males in the hormonal throes of puberty found hell and fast cars a lot more interesting than heaven and slow cars, and thus the Chrysler Hemis became permanently imprinted on tens of millions of adolescent brains. David Grovum, a hot rodder from Grygla, Minnesota, recalls the impression the Hemi made on him when he was a preteen: "The old 392s were extremely vicious cars. An old guy who worked in the creamery in my hometown had a 392 with two four-barrels. I don't know if he ever raced it, but he must have worn out the hood hinges showing off the engine. It was an impressive-looking piece of machinery."

A decade later, when millions of baby boomers found themselves torn away from their hometowns to be sent to the jungles of Vietnam, the national zeitgeist played an even more important role in mythologizing the Hemi. Grovum was one of the young men whose budding love affairs with American performance cars were interrupted by an Uncle Sam–sponsored overseas excursion. "You got some guy laying up in a hooch in Southeast Asia reading those Mopar ads, seeing those quarter-mile times," Grovum says. "He's going to want one of those cars when he comes home."

Colin Comer, one of the world's foremost muscle-car experts and founder of Colin's Classic Cars, an exotic car dealership in Milwaukee, Wisconsin, partly attributes the iconic status of the Hemi engine to its exclusivity. "It was an astronomically expensive engine to build," Comer says, referring to the 426-cubic-inch Hemi (though the original Hemi of the 1950s was also prohibitively expensive to produce). Even though checking the Hemi option on the order sheet could increase the price of a car by up to 50 percent, the Hemi of the 1960s was a loss leader— it cost the company more to build the engines than it charged customers to buy them, and Chrysler lost money producing the 426s. But profit wasn't the point of the 426 Street Hemi; Chrysler only sold the engines to customers in order to qualify them for various forms of racing.

The prices Chrysler charged for street Hemis helped elevate the engine to a mythological status. "You pay $830 for an engine option, you expect it to be fast," Comer says. "A 440 Six-Pack was a lot better motor out of the box—it would easily run with a Hemi, and it cost $500 less. That would buy a lot of gas, but if a guy is intent on buying the fastest car a dealer offers and he sees that one engine costs $500 more than another, he naturally assumes the more expensive engine has to be faster."

"A CASTRATED BULL"

In the reality of the American stoplight drag race (as opposed to the reality of the spec sheet in a car magazine), a strong-running 440 would outrun a bone-stock Hemi, at least in the quarter mile. "You didn't want to race a Hemi past a quarter mile," David Grovum says. To buy a Hemi

LEFT: Zora Arkus-Duntov and his brother Yura developed their Ardun kit that converted the Ford flathead V-8 into an overhead-valve configuration, improving volumetric efficiency.

BELOW: The Ardun heads featured hemispherical combustion chambers.

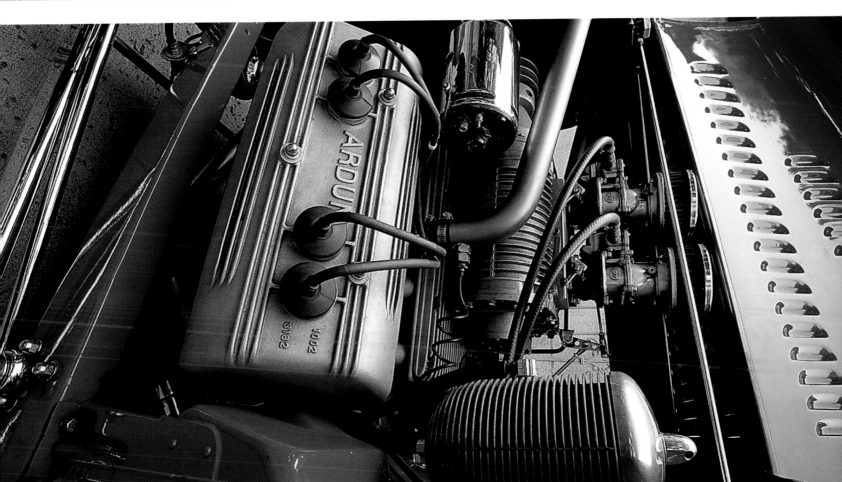

in the 1960s required real commitment: not only the initial financial commitment but the commitment to spend the money and do the finishing work required to bring the engine to its full potential.

Craig Buness, a hot rodder from Crookston, Minnesota, says, "The street Hemi had the most potential of any engine ever sold to the public. But as they came from the factory, they were castrated bulls. The Hemis were basically unfinished race engines. Hemis were select-fit engines, because Chrysler knew how owners were going to use them. All production motors have tolerance variations—you can get a real loose one or a real tight one. A special low-production engine like a Hemi has minimal variation. An engine like that will burn some oil, but it will be the best raw material available for building a race engine."

The problem was converting that raw material into a usable engine. "Your average mechanic at a Chrysler dealership, he knew how to rebuild a slant-six" Buness continues. "He didn't know anything about dual-carb, solid-lifter Hemis. A dealer mechanic would do more harm than good working on a high-performance engine like that."

Even specialty shops sometimes had a hard time coaxing performance out of a Hemi. Buness had a drag racer friend from North Dakota who raced a Hemi. "He bought a yellow-and-black Super Bee. He heard Mr. Norm's ad on the radio: 'You getting your ass handed to you? Come on down to Grand Spaulding and see Mr. Norm. Make sure you ask for the 4.10 rear end.' Glen went to Chicago and said, 'I'm getting beat by 396 Chevelles. What do I have to do?' He had his car dyno-tuned, put on a set of headers, put in 4.10 gears, and came back to town thinking he'd have the fastest car around. And he got beat. It was embarrassing."

The North Dakotan Hemi owner's experience was fairly typical, but that was by design. Larry Ohren, owner of Pennington County Performance, a shop in Thief River Falls, Minnesota, that specializes in Mopar restoration and customization, says, "Chrysler didn't care if the engines underperformed as delivered, because most of the people buying them shouldn't have been buying them in the first place. The people who needed to know how to make a Hemi perform knew how to make a Hemi perform."

Though the Super Bee lacked the distinctive *beep-beep* horn of the Road Runner, it packed the same potent engine options.

Given all the challenges and expense involved with owning and racing a Hemi, it's amazing that the engine enjoyed any popularity at all, much less became an automotive icon. An exorbitant retail price, success in the hands of professional race teams, and untapped performance potential can't completely explain the rise of the Hemi into the realm of the mythological.

Colin Comer believes that the engine itself is the final component of the Hemi's rise to mythic status. "The engine has presence," Comer says. "It has visual impact. You open the hood, it's all motor. It has the perception of speed. You look at it and think, 'That's why this fucker cost $830.'"

BIRTH OF MYTHOS

By the time Chrysler introduced its first passenger cars with V-8 engines, the company's engineers already knew a thing or two about hemispherical combustion chambers. They began experimenting with hemispherical heads on the company's six-cylinder engines almost as soon as Walter Percy Chrysler founded the company in the 1920s. This work eventually led to the Hemi-6 series, a family of six-cylinder engines produced by Chrysler Australia.

During World War II, Chrysler developed a V-16 aircraft engine with hemispherical combustion chambers. Conservatively rated at 2,500 horsepower, in reality the engine produced well over 3,000 horsepower—enough to propel a P-47 Thunderbolt fighter to a speed of 504 miles per hour at 15,000 feet. The powerplant showed great promise, but only a few test units were built before the war ended and development money dried up.

Chrysler wasn't the only company to experiment with hemi heads in the mid-1940s. During the war, Ford shipped a bunch of trucks to England with engines that were so weak "they wouldn't pull a sick whore out of church," according to Grovum. Ford contracted a brilliant young engineer named Zora Arkus-Duntov to develop an overhead-valve conversion kit for the side-valve engines used in the trucks. Arkus-Duntov and his brother, Yura, designed a set of aluminum heads with hemispherical combustion chambers for the anemic flathead Ford. The war had ended by the time the Arkus-Duntov brothers had the heads ready for use, so they lost their military market and instead sold the heads to the budding hot-rod market under the brand-name Ardun. Because of the relatively crude state of metallurgy at the time, these heads suffered from problems caused by different metals expanding at different rates, but their performance showed the design had great promise.

Chrysler had become an extremely conservative company following the spectacular failure of its Airflow automobiles of the 1930s. Walter P. Chrysler had gambled everything on the radical Airflow design, introduced for the 1934 model year; when the car flopped spectacularly, he nearly lost the company that bears his name.

Chrysler, a flamboyant character with a sharp tongue, a short temper, and a predilection for grandiosity, started life as a farm laborer and worked his way up to become the president of Buick. From there, he went on to form his eponymous automobile company, and by 1926

OPPOSITE: The Airflow models were powered by flathead inline eight- and six-cylinder engines (shown here). Side-valve flatheads were the U.S. auto industry standard at the time.

FOLLOWING PAGES: After the spectacular failure of the innovative Airflow models, Chrysler became a pathologically conservative company.

Chrysler Corporation was the third-largest automobile manufacturer in America, behind only General Motors and Ford. Chrysler was justifiably a self-confident man. His hubris undoubtedly contributed to the disastrous decision to bet the future of his company on the Airflows, but the cars themselves had a lot to recommend them. The Airflows had been groundbreaking designs, with such modern features as aerodynamic shapes formed in a wind tunnel, hydraulic brakes, and tubular-steel space frames covered with steel body panels. Unfortunately, the reliability of these advanced cars suffered because they'd been rushed into production at the insistence of Chrysler himself, a decision that diminished any notion of his own infallibility. Between spotty quality control and a shocking design that failed to find acceptance in the marketplace, sales were dismal. The Airflow debacle sent Chrysler Corporation into an economic tailspin that would continue for several years after Walter Chrysler's death in 1940. Not until the immediate postwar years did the company finally recover.

Worse yet, this failure wasn't just disastrous for Chrysler Corporation's bottom line; it also demoralized the company's management. Fearful of a repeat of the Airflow catastrophe, Chrysler executives became extremely cautious and conservative.

The man who succeeded Walter Chrysler in 1935 epitomized this risk-averse mindset. Kaufman Thuma (K. T.) Keller may have learned the lessons of the Airflow too well: his adherence to time-tested automotive design would prove to be almost as financially disastrous as the Airflow experiment. Suffice it to say, with Keller at the helm, the Chrysler Corporation of the 1940s was not an organization prone to taking chances.

Airflow styling was too far ahead of its time for the cars to be accepted in the U.S. marketplace, and their failure nearly spelled the end of Chrysler Corporation.

Keller may have resisted change in any form, but after the war, even the most hidebound Chrysler executive knew the company needed something more than the antiquated side-valve inline sixes and eights that had powered its passenger cars until that point. Styling hadn't changed after the war—like the other major US automakers (with the notable exception of Studebaker), Chrysler continued to build the same basic cars it had built before the war with only minor styling tweaks, such as revised grilles and chrome ornamentation. The automakers used this quick and easy approach in an effort to amortize the costs of the dies and assembly lines they had built earlier in the decade. They could get away with this because they were enjoying a kind of seller's market that had rarely, if ever, been seen before in history.

From 1942 to 1945, the US government had placed a ban on civilian car production. When the ban was finally lifted in late 1945, US buyers were so hungry for new cars to replace their worn-out jalopies that they happily bought just about anything the automakers built.

But while styles didn't change in the immediate postwar years, the market did. In fact, it exploded. Families were growing larger and more affluent, and they needed larger cars to transport the prodigious number of children they were creating in the aftermath of the war. Bigger cars needed more powerful engines, so Chrysler assigned an engine development team that included James Zeder, Ray White, Mel Carpentier, John Platner, and William Drinkard the task of developing a modern engine. Ev Moeller, one of the first people to graduate from the Chrysler Institute in 1939, joined the team in 1947. Moeller had worked in the aircraft engine development program during the war and was familiar with the potential of hemispherical combustion chambers.

Walter Percy Chrysler's gamble on the Airflow models proved a bust, despite their forward styling. Walter Chrysler is seen here with a 1924 model-year automobile, a decade before the introduction of the Airflow.

In the years that followed, the team tested engines from around the world and found that a small four-cylinder built by the English manufacturer Healey had the best power-to-displacement ratio of any powerplant they tested. The Healey featured two camshafts mounted high in the block, pushing short pushrods that operated a pair of valves opening into a hemispherical combustion chamber. Testing conducted by John Platner showed that the hemi design had superior volumetric and thermal efficiency—that is, the domed shape of the combustion chamber maximized the thrusting force created by the combustion process while minimizing the loss of power through heat transference. This allowed the use of higher compression ratios without causing detonation, making the design far more efficient than the side-valve design used in Chrysler's production-car engines. In a paper presented to the Society of Automotive Engineers in 1951, James Zeder wrote:

Throughout all this test work, the hemispherical combustion chamber consistently developed the highest efficiency of all the many designs tested. In other words, this chamber was able to put to work more of the heat energy available in the fuel than could any other production passenger car engine in America . . . Equally important to the high performance of the FirePower engine is the exceptional breathing capacity of this hemispherical chamber design. The cross-section of a FirePower cylinder shows the many features that are conducive to high volumetric efficiency,

or breathing. The valves are not crowded together, nor are they surrounded closely by combustion chamber walls. Both ports are ideally streamlined with a minimum of directional change. The complete separation of the ports, together with the wide space between the valve seats, assures that the incoming charge picks up a minimum of heat from the hot exhaust. In addition, the flow within the cylinder is not restricted by any barriers or tortuous passes.

THE OHC HEMI-6

The team first tested the hemi design on the A161, an inline-six engine they modified to accept hemispherical heads. They used double overhead cams to operate the valves, which was standard practice on many of the high-performance hemi engines being built in Europe at the time. In testing, the engine ran smoothly and produced impressive power, even on the 80-octane pump gas commonly available at the time, but the wide angle of the valves required a complex twin-chain cam drive. While this too was a standard design in Europe, the engineering team believed such a system was too maintenance intensive for the average American car buyer, as well as too expensive to manufacture. The group decided to pursue a different design.

The engineers knew that Cadillac and Oldsmobile were developing overhead-valve (OHV) V-8 engines, and they didn't want Chrysler to be caught with its corporate pants down, so team leader William Drinkard proposed that Chrysler build its own high-performance V-8s—V-8s with hemispherical combustion chambers. Drinkard's proposal hit the company's headquarters in Highland Park, Michigan, like a Molotov cocktail. Chrysler vice chairman Fred Zeder (who happened to be James Zeder's older brother) believed that there was no reason to deviate from the successful inline engine architecture that had served the company so well up until that point. As head of Chrysler's engine development since the formation of the company, the elder Zeder presented a formidable obstacle to making the Hemi V-8 engine a reality.

In 1948, after much corporate infighting that included a fair amount of bickering between the Zeder siblings, the normally risk-averse Keller ended all the arguments and gave the hemispherical-head V-8 project his blessing. Yet even without formal approval, Drinkard's team had been developing an OHV V-8 engine on the sly since the war ended, continuing development work begun during the war. Within weeks they had the A182, a prototype 330-cubic-inch V-8 with hemispherical heads, running on a dynamometer.

The A182 produced impressive power, and Drinkard received permission to develop a production version. Mel Carpentier put together a team that took the next step, building a production prototype of the Hemi engine, the A239. More compact than the A182 (even though displacement increased slightly, to 331 cubic inches), the A239 was built with manufacturing considerations as the utmost priority.

Beyond power, the engineering team also emphasized durability in the new V-8. Drinkard insisted that the engine last at least 100,000 miles without needing to have major components such as pistons, rings, and bearings replaced. But despite such lofty goals, the A239 and subsequent prototype engines suffered from catastrophic camshaft failures. The profiles of the cam lobes loaded stress into the valves; when these loads were transferred back into the cam lobes, it caused the lobe surfaces to disintegrate.

The failures were a result of the team's inexperience in developing overhead-valve engines. To solve the problem, Bob Rodger and a team of engineers worked long hours to develop a reliable camshaft. Rodger, the son of a New York dairy-farming family, earned a master's degree from Chrysler's Institute of Engineering in 1941 and became the head of Chrysler division's engineering department in 1952. The fix involved using graphite-coated tappets and required developing an entirely new manufacturing process. Rodger's team also specified the use of additives in the engine oil to ensure camshaft reliability.

The location of the spark plugs also presented a challenge to the designers. While ideal for fast and efficient combustion, the centrally located spark plugs were difficult to access without removing valve covers. To resolve the issue, the engine design team ran steel tubes through the covers down to the spark plug ports. O-ring seals kept debris out of the cylinder heads and oil inside of them. Long ceramic boots covered the plugs, and the plug wires ran beneath a metal cover to the back of the engine. The result was a clean, purposeful-looking engine that appeared elegant and brutish at the same time. In addition to being the most powerful engine of its day, the new Hemi would also be the most handsome.

Given the performance potential of the engine, the engineering team specified heavy-duty parts throughout, such as shot-peened forged-steel crankshafts that spun in five main bearings. Since the engine was being developed for use in luxury sedans rather than high-performance sports cars, ease of maintenance took precedence over raw power, and the new engine used hydraulic lifters instead of solid units, lowering the rev limit of the engine but eliminating the need for periodic valve adjustments.

Chrysler teamed up with Carter to develop a two-barrel carburetor that featured an integral water jacket to prevent the carb from icing up in cold weather. To make the engine more user friendly, it also featured an automatic choke. A lot of spark would be needed to extract the potential power from the Hemi design, so the team specified a dual-breaker ignition system.

The Airflow's failure would have repercussions for Chrysler. K. T. Keller showed an aversion to risk as Chrysler's president from 1935 to 1950, and later as its chairman.

2

The Proto-Muscle Cars

After extensive dyno and road testing, the Hemi engine was production ready by midyear 1950. By that time, the OHV V-8 competition from Oldsmobile and Cadillac had been on the market for two years—Cadillac introduced its V-8 in October 1948 and Oldsmobile's Rocket V-8 followed its corporate cousin to the market one month later. The GM V-8s had already developed a following, both on the country's racetracks and in the marketplace. For the newcomer from Chrysler to win customers away from the General Motors divisions, the new Hemi had to be more than good; it had to be the best engine available in any American car dealership.

It was. The engine, under the name FirePower, featured a compression ratio of 7.5:1 and had a 1.81-inch intake valve and a 1.5-inch exhaust valve. It arrived at its 331.1-cubic-inch displacement through a cylinder bore of 3.8125 inches and a stroke of 3.625 inches. This made the engine an oversquare design (the bore was larger than the stroke). The primary advantage of such a design is a shorter stroke for

OPPOSITE: Chrysler offered the Hemi engine as an option on the Saratoga Club Coupe, making it the first car to use the muscle-car formula: potent V-8 power in a mid-sized two-door.

ABOVE: **Cadillac introduced the modern American overhead-valve V-8 in the Coupe de Ville.**

RIGHT AND OPPOSITE: **Oldsmobile followed Cadillac into the world of V-8 muscle with the Rocket 88.**

a given displacement, resulting in slower piston speeds—a piston traveling up and down a 3.6-inch cylinder bore at 2,000 rpm is covering a lot less ground than a piston traveling at the same rate in a 4-inch cylinder bore. The end result is an engine that can run reliably at higher rpm while at the same time living a longer life thanks to less wear and tear on the pistons, rings, rods, bearings, crankshaft, and cylinder bore at normal operating speeds.

Compared to the 330.0-cubic-inch Cadillac V-8 and 303.7-cubic-inch Olds Rocket engine, the new Hemi was remarkably efficient. The downside was that the Hemi heads were heavy: a pair weighed 120 pounds versus the 94-pound weight of a pair of Cadillac cylinder heads. Chrysler engineers compensated by keeping the weight of other components down, so both the Cadillac and Chrysler engines weighed about the same, around 700 pounds. Both engines used a 7.5:1 compression ratio, but the Hemi produced 180 horsepower, besting the Cadillac's 160 horsepower and the Olds' 135 horsepower by a good margin and proving the superiority of hemispherical combustion chambers when it came to producing raw

The New Thrill IN PERFORMANCE
OLDSMOBILE "ROCKET"

Here it is—Oldsmobile's revolutionary, Valve-in-Head, High-Octane, "Rocket" Engine! Designed to match the superlative styling of the Futuramic car, this new power plant is here this year in the Futuramic Oldsmobile "88" and "98" Series. The "Rocket" is all new in concept and design—the source of the most sensational highway action you've ever known. You've got to try it to believe it! It's Oldsmobile's "New Thrill!"

Make a Date with a "Rocket 8"!

"88"

THE BIG NUMBER WITH THE NEW LOW PRICE FOR 1950

The hottest number on the highway—
the most talked about car in America—
that's the famous Oldsmobile "88"!
Now at an even lower price for 1950!
"Rocket" Engine action—most thrilling ever!
Futuramic styling—fleet, smart, distinctive!
Whirlaway Hydra-Matic*—superbly smooth!
Now all yours at the lowest cost ever!
Take a demonstration drive tomorrow.
Just call your Oldsmobile dealer and . . .
make a date with a "Rocket 8"!

Compare it with any other car on the road
for performance—for driving ease—
for *value*. You'll be dollars ahead when
you rocket ahead in Oldsmobile's "88"—
at 1950's new low price!

A General Motors Value

*Whirlaway Hydra-Matic Drive,
at reduced price, now optional
on all Oldsmobile models.

OLDSMOBILE

ABOVE: While Chrysler had an earth-shattering engine design, its cars were still frumpy and old fashioned.

LEFT: General Motors lit a fire in the performance world with its overhead-valve V-8 engines. When Chrysler introduced the Hemi engines, they dropped an atomic bomb.

horsepower. (Torque figures of the FirePower and Cadillac V-8 were identical, at 312 pound-feet apiece.)

This was years before the horsepower wars that took place a decade later, when engines were producing close to 500 horsepower; in the fall of 1950, 180 horsepower was an astounding number. It certainly made an impression on a young hot rodder from Florida named Donald Glenn Garlits. Recalling the first time he saw "180 horsepower" posted on a sign advertising the new Hemi in a Chrysler dealership window, the man who later became much better known as "Big Daddy" Don Garlits assumed that the dealer had made a mistake and had transposed the last two digits. It seemed to him and his friends that 108 horsepower was a lot more probable.

SARATOGA CLUB COUPE MUSCLE

Chrysler made the FirePower standard equipment on the New Yorker and Imperial models and offered it as an extra-cost option on the Saratoga. The Windsor model soldiered on with the old inline side-valve engines. With their new Hemi engines, these first three were the fastest luxury cars on the market, but none of them competed directly with the Rocket 88, which Oldsmobile had created by mounting its Rocket V-8 in its lighter 88 chassis. The Rocket 88 was the proto–muscle car. Chrysler responded by introducing a 1952 model that would take full advantage of the new Hemi: the Saratoga Club Coupe. Rather than being a two-door version of the heavy Saratoga sedan, the Club Coupe used the lighter Windsor chassis. Chrysler might have been following Oldsmobile's lead by putting its hottest engine in its lightest chassis, but out on the street the 180-horsepower Club Coupe smoked the 135-horsepower Rocket 88.

Once the engine was bolted into a midsized chassis, the superiority of the Hemi quickly made itself known on the street. When *Road & Track* tested a Saratoga Club Coupe with a FirePower Hemi mounted in its engine bay for its November 1951 issue, the magazine got the car from 0 to 60 miles per hour in 10 seconds flat. The Cadillac Coupe de Ville took 13.5 seconds to get to 60; the Rocket 88 took 12.5 seconds to accomplish the same. The magazine described the testing procedure it used to achieve its impressive results: "With the selector in low range the clutch was disengaged and the engine revved to about 25 percent throttle (normal starts do not require use of clutch) . . ."

The Firepower Hemi engine provided Indianapolis Chrysler dealership C. H. Wallerich with the fodder for exciting ad copy. As did the fact a Chrysler New Yorker paced the 1951 Indianapolis 500 (see following page).

The Hemi-powered Chrysler New Yorker that served as the 1951 Indianapolis 500 pace car.

Depressing the throttle any more than 25 percent made the Chrysler sit still and peel rubber, losing precious split seconds . . . Then with the engine winding to the proper point, the clutch was sharply engaged. At about 35 mph the clutch was again floored, and the throttle was held "full on." This put the 3rd gear into play and at around 65 mph the throttle was again backed off to allow the car to drop to 4th. When this is performed in proper sequence a 0–60 time of 10 seconds should result.

Road & Track, a magazine that has always favored European sporting hardware over more pedestrian American transportation devices, couldn't hide its enthusiasm for the new Hemi-powered Chrysler:

Road & Track's test crew seldom gets excited about American cars, but then *Road & Track* readers are familiar with this attitude. The Chrysler is an exception. While it has faults, and some of them are serious, we feel that it is outstanding among local efforts . . . The tremendous performance of this V-8 is enough in itself to be a strong selling point for the Chrysler. Regardless of the rest of the car's advantages or disadvantages, when you touch that throttle, you know something mighty impressive is happening under that hood.

RIGHT: The Hemi-powered DeSoto that paced the 1956 Indianapolis 500 featured on the cover and inside of that June's *Hot Rod* magazine.

BELOW: A Dodge Royal paced the 1954 Indianapolis 500, with Jerry Lewis and Dean Martin taking a spin in the yellow convertible. A factory-installed four-barrel on an Offenhauser intake raised output of the Red Ram Hemi from the standard 150 horsepower to 200.

TESTING A NEW TYPE SUPERCHARGER

HOT ROD
The Automotive [...] magazine

BIG GEARS
for your FORD

RODDERS WIN
in Mobilgas
ECONOMY RUN

JUNE 1956 25c

HRM REPORTS:
'56 INDY PACE CAR—HOTTEST **DRAG SEDAN**

Road & Track wasn't the only publication to rave about the Hemi's performance. In a *Motor Trend* comparison test of fifteen cars from the 1951 model year, the Chrysler V-8 beat the second-place Oldsmobile V-8 by a score of 176 to 153.5 points. The magazine concluded, "It cost the Chrysler Corporation a lot of money to build the new V-8; it took a lot of courage to flout tradition and experiment with design. The award winner is, in concept, a major step ahead in American automotive history."

NASCAR

At the same time, the Hemi was already on its way to becoming a legend on the racetrack: America's dirt ovals were the setting of the new and increasingly popular sport of stock-car racing—that is, races in which stock-bodied production cars competed. This all-American form of racing had its base in the southeastern quadrant of the country, thanks to an enterprising mechanic named William France Sr. who had moved from Washington, DC, to Daytona Beach, Florida, during the Great Depression. France hatched a scheme to turn stock-car racing into a profitable business. In 1948, together with a group of racers and promoters, France created the National Association for Stock Car Automobile Racing (NASCAR) Grand National series. A hot production engine like Chrysler's new Hemi was tailor-made for this type of racing.

By the time of the Hemi's debut, NASCAR racing had grown so popular it was expanding out beyond its Southern roots. On August 12, 1951, the budding series came to Detroit for the first time, in the form of

ABOVE: Raw driving talent and a Hemi-powered racer probably contributed to Lee Petty's success at least as much as his Champion sparkplugs did.

LEFT: Though the DeSoto brand would soon disappear off the face of the Earth, the Hemi engine powering it had only just begun its reign.

OPPOSITE: Lee Petty dominated the NASCAR race on the Daytona Beach road course in 1954, leading 37 of the 39 laps.

SHOWCASE OF 1953 FOREIGN CARS — Photos! Specifications!

MOTOR TREND

The Car Owners Magazine

JANUARY 1953
25¢

ROAD TEST:
POWER-PACKED '53 DODGE V-8

CUSTOM or CLASSIC — THE GREAT DEBATE!

LEFT AND BELOW: The Hemi engine trickled down to the Dodge brand by 1953. *Motor Trend* wasn't being hyperbolic when it described the new Dodge Hemi as "power-packed."

OPPOSITE AND FOLLOWING PAGES: The Saratoga might have looked like a car from an earlier era, but the fact that it weighed 250 pounds less than a New Yorker meant that it made better use of the Hemi engine. In fact, Bill Sterling drove this nearly stock Saratoga to a first-in-class and third-overall finish in the 1951 La Carrera Panamericana road race.

1953 DODGE V-8 CORONET SEDAN

This easy-to-drive, compact car further indicates a trend with its V-8 engine

An MT Research Report by Walt Woron and Jim Potter

Photos by Jack Campbell

Lester Lum "Tex" Colbert knew that Chrysler needed to modernize the design of its cars or go out of business.

the inaugural Motor City 250. Held on a 1-mile dirt track at the Michigan State Fairgrounds near the intersection of Woodward Avenue and Eight Mile Road, this race marked the first time that many auto industry executives would be able to see Bill France's NASCAR extravaganza in all of its whiskey-tripping glory.

It also marked the first ever NASCAR Grand National win for a Hemi-powered Chrysler. Tommy Thompson, an engineer from Louisville, Kentucky, took the checkered flag in a New Yorker coupe, beating Curtis Turner in a Rocket 88. Watching the epic battle between Turner and Thompson—complete with Turner's Olds giving Thompson's Chrysler a little love tap, sending both drivers temporarily off the track—ignited a great deal of interest in factory NASCAR participation.

Almost overnight, the new Chrysler engine stirred interest from all levels of motorsports. A New Yorker convertible was selected as the pace car for the 1951 Indianapolis 500. This would be the first of several Hemi-powered cars that would pace the fabled Memorial Day Classic—in 1954 a Dodge Royal 500 paced the race, and in 1956 a DeSoto Pacesetter held the honor.

Further south, La Carrera Panamericana (the Mexican Road Race, or Pan Am) was another event that allowed drivers to capitalize on the power of Chrysler's amazing new engine. The Mexican government organized the race, which was so popular that in 1954 it constituted one-fourth of the World Sportscar Championship (along with the Mille Miglia in Italy, the 24-Hours Nürburgring in Germany, and the 24 Hours of Le Mans in France). First held in 1950, La Carrera Panamericana took place in nine stages along a 2,176-mile stretch of the newly completed Pan American Highway. In 1951 Bill Sterling drove a nearly bone-stock Saratoga to a first-in-class finish, and third overall, behind a pair of Ferraris.

Despite this promising start, Chryslers didn't fare well in the next two Pan Ams. Lincoln had introduced a new OHV V-8 for 1952, and Lincolns won the stock-car class in 1952 and 1953. Chrysler again took top honors in the small stock-car class (the stock car division had been subdivided between passenger cars, small US stock cars, and European stock cars) when Tommy Drisdale won in a Dodge. The year 1954 marked the last time the incredibly dangerous race would be run. The era of racing on public roads was coming to an end.

Unfortunately, Chrysler was unable to capitalize on the excitement over the new Hemi engine. Not even a world-beating engine could pull the company out of the mud that was the 1952 model year. Chrysler had coasted on its prewar styling for far too long. By the early 1950s, all the US automakers that were still viable were producing cars with styling that made Chrysler's offerings look like the warmed-over prewar boxes they were. While other manufacturers' dealerships received modern-looking cars for the 1952 model year, Chrysler dealers were stuck with cars that looked exactly like the 1951 models, their only stylistic update consisting of new taillight surrounds. (To be fair, the new taillights did incorporate back-up lights.)

This lack of change was, in part, by design; Chrysler used the 1952 model year to synchronize its new releases with the rest of the industry and in a way wrote off the entire model year. Ever since the war had ended, the company had been introducing new models during the calendar year in which they were labeled. Meanwhile, all the other automakers were unveiling their new cars three months earlier, in the fall of the previous year, as was the tradition for the US auto market. For the 1952 model year, Chrysler deliberately didn't put much effort into restyling cars that were destined to be something very much like sacrificial goats.

As it turned out, 1952 would be the year Chrysler finally paid the price for its conservative-to-the-point-of-regressive approach. K. T. Keller may have gone against his character when he had personally approved the Hemi engine project, but when it came to styling and design, he kept a death grip on the corporate purse strings. In 1952, the American car-buying public made the consequences of this folly painfully clear. In 1951 Chrysler division sold 162,916 cars; in 1952 that number fell to 120,678. Clearly, change was needed. Fortunately, that change had already begun to take place, in the form of Tex Colbert and Virgil Exner.

ADVANCED STYLING

Lester Lum "Tex" Colbert began his career as a lawyer, working for a firm used by Walter P. Chrysler. He and Chrysler hit it off, and Colbert eventually became the president of Chrysler's Dodge division. K. T. Keller shared his predecessor's enthusiasm for Colbert. In fact, as Keller neared retirement, he groomed Colbert to be his replacement. Following the outbreak of the Korean War in 1950, the Pentagon selected Keller to head the

Colbert hired Virgil Exner to bring cutting-edge design to Chrysler.

US missile program, and on November 3, 1950, Colbert assumed the reins of Chrysler Corporation. Keller remained on, however, as the chairman of Chrysler's board, a position that had remained vacant since Walter P. Chrysler's death in 1940.

Colbert knew the company needed to supplant its stodgy prewar designs with modern automobiles, so his first order of business was to order the immediate redesign of all passenger cars. Unfortunately, the realities of manufacturing automobiles dictate that "immediately" translates to three or four years down the road—and that's in the best of circumstances. Thanks to Keller's slavish devotion to stylistic entropy, Colbert's position hardly qualified as the best of circumstances.

All was not completely lost, however, because Colbert's staff already had just the man to lead Chrysler into the era of modern design. The year before he stepped down, K. T. Keller had hired a brilliant designer named Virgil Exner. With an eye toward the future, Keller set Exner up in an advanced styling studio, giving him the opportunity to work relatively free of the constraints placed on stylists by the company's engineers. Walter P. Chrysler had always appreciated good engineers, placing them in most of the top executive positions within his company. By the early 1950s, engineering's power over styling generally took the form of Henry King, who was responsible for production designs at the time Exner came on board.

In almost every way, Exner was the perfect man to implement Colbert's directive to take Chrysler styling in a new direction. From 1934 until 1938, he'd headed Pontiac's design department, working for Harley Earl, who is generally considered to be the founder of automotive design. In 1938 he went to work for Raymond Loewy, whose firm designed everything from Lucky Strike cigarette packages to Greyhound buses. At Loewy, Exner designed cars for Studebaker. In 1947 Raymond Loewy fired him for designing Studebaker's new 1947 models behind Loewy's back; Exner had actually been working at the insistence of the firm's client, who believed Loewy's interference would keep the redesign from being finished on time. Whatever the circumstances, Exner found himself in the position of freelance designer, and Keller hired him in 1949.

Loewy might not have been pleased with Exner's work on the 1947 Studebakers, but everyone else was. When they hit the moribund postwar US auto market, their futuristic styling motivated other manufactures to develop modern designs.

Exner took a Gestalt approach to designing automobiles. He believed in working with the car as a unit, rather than a collection of parts. In a presentation to the Society of Automotive Engineers on January 14–15, 1952, Exner summed up this approach:

An automobile cannot be properly styled unless it is first conceived as a whole unit . . . The theme must be a single one to which all components are intimately related. Concentration on various parts such as fenders, tops, front end, etc., is not possible until the overall picture is clearly established.

The 1952 Chryslers might have been shockingly status quo, but that didn't mean Exner was sitting on his stylistic thumbs. His influence on product design was minimal in the early years, because Henry King and his engineering staff viewed Exner as a usurper and severely limited his design input. It was because of King's attempt to marginalize Exner that the advanced design studio was located offsite. In a way, this was the best thing that could have happened to Exner and to Chrysler. Without the constraints of designing cars for production, Exner was free to create the ultimate expressions of his design aesthetic. Together with Maury Baldwin and Cliff Voss, Exner's little advanced design studio created cars that represented genuine

Virgil Exner's K-310 show car was as stylish as the cars Chrysler was trying to sell in its showrooms were stodgy.

breakthroughs in automotive design. Exner and company used this creative freedom to build a series of one-off cars that would travel to Chrysler dealerships around the country, showing dealers and customers alike that the company would eventually produce something other than the prewar transportation boxes currently taking up space on showroom floors.

The first of those advanced design exercises to become a chrome-and-steel reality was the K-310, which Exner's team designed in Detroit but was built by Carrozzeria Ghia in Turin, Italy. This was in part to ensure secrecy and keep the project off King's radar, but the farming out of the K-310 project was also the result of Chrysler's devoting all available resources to military production because of the ongoing war in Korea.

This stylish four-seat sports coupe proved a rolling prototype for the design sensibility that Exner would bring to Chrysler's sporty production cars in a few short years. In the previously mentioned presentation to the Society of Automotive Engineers, Exner described the influences that had shaped his vision of the K-310, which he defined as British-traditional, German-functional, French-flamboyant, and Italian-simple. "Sometimes we become too preoccupied with our Detroit designs," Exner told the assembled crowd, "and fail to take note of what the other fellow is doing."

One of the most influential features of the K-310 was its long hood and short rear deck, elements that would come to define the cars of the classic muscle-car era a generation later. Exner extolled the functional virtues of such a design. He believed a long hood allowed better access to the engine compartment and a short deck moved the passenger compartment back, placing more weight on the rear wheels for better traction and balance. He also understood the effect a long hood and short deck had on people viewing the design. In his January 1952 speech to the Society of Automotive Engineers, he explained: "The long hood is a potent psychological factor in that it denotes power and strong directional quality."

That, and it just plain looks cool. Ford would adopt this design for its Mustang production car a dozen years after Exner's speech and, in so doing, would dictate the expectations of performance car buyers from that point forward.

THE HOT ROD BOYS

James Zeder, who became Chrysler's vice president of engineering in 1951, when his brother Fred died, initially showed little more interest in developing the Hemi's vast reserves of untapped performance potential than K. T. Keller and Henry King showed in developing updated body styles. But engineers are engineers, and ultimately Zeder became infected with the enthusiasm generated by the group of engineers whom he called "the hot rod boys." Zeder gave engineering the go-ahead to experiment with high-performance versions of the Hemi.

OPPOSITE: The K-310's style extended beyond the exterior to beneath the hood.

They began by raising compression ratios. With no other changes but a bump in the compression ratio to 12.5:1, they coaxed 228 horsepower from a stock 331 engine, but that required the use of fuel with an octane rating of 130 or better. This route was out of the question, because Zeder dictated that all production versions of the engine would run on regular pump gas. As he'd told the Society of Automotive Engineers in 1951:

We at Chrysler Corporation are in favor of increasing compression ratios as fast as higher-octane fuels become commercially available. In the interests of economy and savings to the consumer, we intend in the future to use the highest compression which will permit smooth operation with regularly available fuels. But at the same time we intend to pursue all other avenues of increasing engine performance and economy . . . The hemispherical combustion chamber not only makes [the Hemi engine] the most efficient engine available today (in terms of pounds of fuel used per brake horsepower hour), but it also makes it better able to take advantage of better fuels [that] will be developed in the future.

The development team began working on a version of the engine that had better flow into and out of the combustion chambers. This engine—dubbed the K-310, the same moniker given to Exner's styling exercise of the same period—featured a set of tuned tubular headers in place of the stock Hemi's exhaust manifolds, leading to an increase of 13 horsepower (to 193) and 18 pound-feet of torque (to 330).

They polished the intake and exhaust ports and installed bigger valves, with 2.06-inch valves in the intake ports and 1.625-inch valves in the exhaust ports. They developed a manifold that allowed the use of four one-barrel downdraft carburetors, and they used an electronic computer to determine the ultimate cam profiles. With 7.0:1 compression pistons, the K-310 engine generated 308 horsepower and 361 pound-feet of torque. When 12.5:1 compression pistons were installed, the engine cranked out 353 horsepower and 385 pound-feet of torque. Using the lessons learned from the K-310 test engine, Chrysler bumped the power of the production FirePower engine to 190 for the 1952 model year.

That same year DeSoto introduced a 276-cubic-inch version of the Hemi engine. Like its bigger Chrysler brother, the DeSoto Hemi featured an oversquare bore and stroke ratio, in this case the bore being 3.625 inches and the stroke being 3.440 inches. Intake valves measured 1.84 inches across, and 1.5-inch units served duty in the exhaust ports. With a 7.0:1 compression ratio and a two-barrel carburetor, the DeSoto Hemi pumped out 160 horsepower and 250 pound-feet of torque. With the advent of the Hemi engine, DeSoto dropped the Deluxe and Custom nameplates from its cars and renamed the six-cylinder version the Powermaster and the V-8 version the Firedome, in honor of its Hemi engine.

In 1953 Dodge introduced its version of the Hemi, the Red Ram. This engine, the smallest version of the original Hemi, at 241 cubic inches, differed quite a bit from

ABOVE: The Cunningham C-2R at the Autodrome de Linas, Montlhéry, France, in 1951.

LEFT: Briggs Cunningham and his Hemi-powered racers earned the coveted cover of *Time* magazine for their April 26, 1954, issue.

APRIL 26, 1954

THE H-BOMB IN COLOR

TIME
THE WEEKLY NEWSMAGAZINE

2

1

ROAD RACER BRIGGS CUNNINGHAM
Horsepower, endurance, sportsmanship.

$6.00 A YEAR

VOL. LXIII NO. 17

its larger brethren. Like the FireDome, it featured a compression ratio of 7.0:1, and like both the DeSoto and Chrysler engines, it used a two-barrel carburetor. But with a bore and stroke of just 3.4375 inches and 3.250 inches, respectively, the combustion chambers were much more compact, requiring the use of smaller valves. The Red Ram used 1.75-inch intake and 1.41-inch exhaust valves.

That same year, Bob Rodger began development of a clandestine project—a sporty car that would mate Virgil Exner's styling to a powerful Hemi engine. The Exner body and Hemi engine would be mounted on a chassis with a sophisticated suspension, giving the car handling prowess to match its looks and acceleration. This would become the C-300.

These Hemis of 1953 were great engines, but by that time the FirePower no longer occupied the top slot in the American V-8 performance hierarchy. That honor belonged to Cadillac, which had increased the output of its OHV V-8 to 210 horsepower. That year Cadillac beat Chrysler in the NASCAR race at Daytona. Even worse for Chrysler, other General Motors divisions were producing V-8 engines that nearly equaled the output of Chrysler's once-dominant Hemi. The Oldsmobile Rocket engine now cranked out 165 horsepower, and Buick had introduced a new OHV V-8 that generated 188 horsepower.

For 1954 Chrysler increased the output of the two-barrel FirePower to 195 horsepower and offered a four-barrel version that produced 235 horsepower. This barely put the Chrysler engine ahead of the Cadillac, which was bumped up to 230 horsepower for the 1954 model year. But all the other manufacturers also increased the outputs of their OHV V-8 engines.

The Buick increased to 200 horsepower, the Olds to 185 horsepower, the DeSoto to 170 horsepower, and the Dodge to 150 horsepower. With an aftermarket manifold manufactured by Offenhauser and sold through Dodge parts departments, output of the Dodge Red Ram could be increased to an estimated 180 horsepower. Even stodgy old Ford was getting in on the act, finally replacing its antiquated side-valve V-8 with a slightly less antiquated OHV engine; this 239-cubic-inch unit generated 130 horsepower.

Chrysler sales suffered from competition and stodgy styling, but the Hemis were still more than competitive on the track. Lee Petty won the Daytona race in 1954, putting the superior power of the Hemi engine in his New Yorker to good use and taking pole position with a qualifying speed of 123.4 miles per hour. (Petty didn't cross the finish line first—Oldsmobile driver Tim Flock took the checkered flag, but Flock's Olds was disqualified when a postrace tech inspection uncovered an illegally modified carburetor.) Petty took first in seven races that season and went on to give Chrysler its first-ever NASCAR Grand National championship.

BRIGGS SWIFT CUNNINGHAM

As powerful as the Hemis were, everyone involved with developing the engine knew the engines could be much more powerful. Given the tremendous untapped potential of the design, it seemed ridiculous to engage in incremental leapfrogging with the other manufacturers when it would be a simple matter to make a Hemi so powerful that it would take the other manufacturers years to catch up. And Chrysler's engineers knew just how to build such an engine, thanks in large part to development work done to help out a racer and sports-car builder named Briggs Cunningham.

In 1907 Briggs Swift Cunningham II was born into a wealthy Cincinnati banking family. His uncle indoctrinated him at an early age him into the cult of motorsports by taking him street racing in a Dodge powered by a Hispano-Suiza aircraft engine. Cunningham became a racing junky and enjoyed a mildly successful career racing sports cars, but he dreamed of something more—his goal was to field a team of American cars with American drivers who would win the fabled 24 Hours of Le Mans race in France.

Cunningham tried to achieve this goal in 1950 by fielding his Fordillac, a Frankenstein creation that mated a Cadillac V-8 with a lightweight Ford chassis. The organizations sanctioning the Le Mans race rejected the car because they didn't consider it a production vehicle, so Cunningham bought two Cadillac Coupe DeVilles to enter in the race. One kept the stock bodywork, but the other featured a body that had been cobbled together by employees of the Grumman aircraft factory.

Cunningham's cars finished tenth and eleventh that year, a result decent enough to earn the respect of French fans, but Cunningham wanted more. He recognized the potential of the Hemi engine and decided to use that powerplant in his new C-2, a car he was building to race at Le Mans in 1951. Cunningham spent a then-staggering

$100,000 to build the car, which featured coil-spring suspension at all four corners and a de Dion independent rear suspension. Unfortunately, the car and the Hemi engine were heavy, weighing about 700 pounds more than the C-2's closest competitors, and Cunningham finished eighteenth overall.

To provide Cunningham with a competitive engine, a team of Chrysler engineers that included John Platner and Don Moore began working on the A311 engine program. This program, which would become the foundation for most of Chrysler's racing engines throughout the 1950s, represented the state of the engine-building art at that time. In its ultimate form, it featured gear-driven camshafts with roller tappets that had extreme lift and duration numbers, a 12:1 compression ratio (no dictates about using pump gas here), aluminum racing pistons, Hilborn fuel injection with tuned velocity stacks, special pushrods, and dual valve springs with surge dampeners. Testing revealed the engine was so strong that it was flexing the block, so the engineering team mounted a bracing plate between the block and the oil pan for added structural rigidity.

Cunningham further developed his cars for 1952, now labeled the C-4Rs, shedding some 600 pounds from the overall weight of the car and engine package. The FirePower engine now generated 300 reliable horsepower. Unfortunately, the five-speed transmissions Cunningham installed in the cars didn't prove as reliable as the engines; they suffered lubrication problems under racing conditions, and Cunningham was forced to substitute Cadillac three-speed transmissions at the last minute. This put the C-4Rs at a tremendous disadvantage when braking down Le Mans's long straights, but even though two of the three cars Cunningham entered broke down and didn't finish the race, the third car, driven by Cunningham himself, finished a respectable fourth.

In 1953 Cunningham had to reduce the compression ratio of the A311 to 7.5:1 in order to use the mandated French gasoline, but he still drove his C-5R to a podium finish, taking third overall. In 1954 Cunningham entered two C-4Rs, each powered by 330-horsepower A311 engines, and his drivers finished third and fifth overall. Cunningham might not have achieved his dream of winning at Le Mans, but he did manage to outrun all but a handful of factory-sponsored teams while trying.

INDIANAPOLIS 500

Chrysler engineers were pleased with Cunningham's results in France, but they had their eyes set on a prize a little closer to home: the Indianapolis 500. They developed a version of the A311 that generated over 400 horsepower. When mounted in a Kurtis Kraft racing chassis, this engine/car combination averaged over 135 miles per hour in testing at the Indianapolis Motor Speedway. The engine was rugged enough for the Memorial Day race too, running for 900 miles at a stretch without needing so much as a change of spark plugs.

These results were perhaps too impressive; they scared the powers that be, and at the last minute the sanctioning bodies lowered the displacement limit for the Indianapolis 500

to 275 cubic inches. Chrysler experimented with a 271-cubic-inch version of the A311 but didn't have enough time to make it competitive.

The engineers got their revenge, though. When Chrysler opened its Chelsea Proving Grounds in 1954, the company invited the top four finishers from that year's Indy 500 to test their cars on the high-banked 4.7-mile track, which allowed drivers to maintain wide-open throttle over the entire course. The fastest lap turned in by the four drivers was 179 miles per hour. Then Chrysler brought out a Kurtis Kraft roadster powered by an A311 racing engine and proceeded to lap the track at 182 miles per hour.

The A311 played another notable role: influencing Tom Hoover, who would go on to become the godfather of the 426 Hemi. In an interview published in the August 2005 issue of *Hot Rod*, Hoover told the magazine:

The thing that was the most significant to me was the A311 program that explored the potential of the Chrysler 331 Hemi as a potential Indianapolis 500 racing engine. The A311 report became the most desirable reading material among those of us enrolled in the Chrysler Institute. I graduated from the Chrysler Institute in 1957 and at about the same time a group of Chrysler employees formed the Ram Chargers group, a loose knit bunch of engineers who drag raced their cars on weekends. Even though the A311 program didn't produce an Indy victory due to USAC rule changes, the technical report it generated was a guiding light for me.

ABOVE: The Hemi engine of a Cunningham C-5R at the 1953 running of the 24 Hours of Le Mans.

FOLLOWING PAGES: The Cunningham C-4R of Bill Spear and Sherwood Johnston at the 1954 running of the 24 Hours of Le Mans.

3

Luxurious Muscle

When the 1955 Chryslers hit the market, one model in the lineup—the C-300—was so groundbreaking that its influence on both performance and styling would be felt for generations to come.

Chrysler was the last company anyone would have pegged to produce such a revolutionary design. While other manufacturers had been changing to suit the times—building cars that were longer, lower, and wider—Chrysler maintained the stately, upright proportions of its prewar cars. It took something akin to an automotive apocalypse to get the company to abandon the boxy styling that K. T. Keller had locked onto like a pit bull on a hambone. That apocalypse came in the form of 1954 sales figures. Total Chrysler sales plummeted from 170,006 cars in 1953 to 104,985 cars in 1954. Dodge and Plymouth numbers were even worse than Chrysler's. The public wanted longer, lower, wider cars, and if Chrysler wouldn't provide them, well, K. T. Keller's minions could drive their old-fart cars straight to hell as fast as their overachieving Hemi engines could carry them.

OPPOSITE: The Adventurer was the most sporting model in Chrysler's DeSoto line for 1956.

When the numbers came in, Keller finally understood that he had been wrong to block design progress at Chrysler. He told the *Detroit Free Press*, "I have seen the error of my ways. Christ, we can't afford another mistake." Chrysler was finally ready to implement some of Virgil Exner's revolutionary styling ideas. In his book *Chrysler & Imperial 1946–1975: The Classic Postwar Years* (Motorbooks, 1975), author Richard M. Langworth recounts a meeting between Keller and Exner, as described by Exner's son, Virgil Jr.:

> There came the day when K. T. Keller asked Dad's opinion on what the 1955 stuff was going to look like. Dad told him "lousy." K. T. kind of liked that—[Keller] was quite a strong character.
>
> "Okay," he said, "you put it together and you've got 18 months." They quickly swiped ideas off the parade cars [Exner's design exercises, or "idea cars," as he called them] and managed to put the 1955 line together in time.

Exner based the styling of the 1955 lineup on the Parade Phaeton, a show car he had created in 1952 using a Crown Imperial chassis. The new models from Chrysler had the long, low, clean lines that customers of the day demanded. The crown jewel in the new line was the C-300, which made its debut on February 8, 1955.

OPPOSITE TOP: The 1955 Chrysler C-300 was the first car to bring together modern style and Hemi power.

OPPOSITE BOTTOM: With its dual four-barrel carburetors and solid lifters, the 331-ci Hemi in the C-300 cranked out 300 horsepower.

BELOW: With 300 horses backing up its name, the C-300 went on to earn many of the checkered flags that adorned its hood emblem.

THE MOST POWERFUL SEDAN IN THE WORLD

Bob Rodger headed the C-300 development team. A serious race fan, Rodger had been inspired to build a more sporting Chrysler by watching the Mexican Race and Briggs Cunningham's cars in the early 1950s. In the first weeks of August 1954, he approached Ed Quinn, the general manager of Chrysler division, about the sporty car project he had been developing on the sly for more than a year.

Quinn told Rodger that he could develop the project but specified that he couldn't deviate in any expensive fashion from the 1955 production models, which were set to hit the showroom in a couple of months. The 1954 disaster had cleared out Chrysler's coffers, forcing the company to borrow operating money from Prudential to survive. Needless to say, there wasn't a lot of fat in the budget for expensive die changes for pet projects. Because of this, the C-300 was a prime example of parts-bin engineering. Exner, Cliff Voss, and Tom Poirier selected a New Yorker hardtop body and Windsor rear quarter panels. The grille, parking lights, and front bumper came from the Imperial. As production neared, Exner made some last-minute tweaks. He replaced the Imperial bumpers—which he considered too bulky for a sporting car—with more slender Chrysler bumpers and parking lights.

Despite being cobbled together from existing components, the C-300 was stunningly beautiful. Apparently, parts-bin engineering works when the parts are as good as those that Exner's team had at their disposal.

While Exner handled styling chores, Rodger concentrated on engine development. His foundation was a stock 331-cubic-inch Hemi block, which had been redesigned for the 1955 model year with altered water passages to improve cooling. To this he added the steep cam from the A311 race engine program and installed solid lifters, 8.5:1 compression pistons, and bigger valves, then mounted a second four-barrel carburetor. The result was the 300-horsepower engine that gave the C-300 its name.

This engine didn't just represent an incremental improvement over the competition; it was a giant leap ahead. No matter how one measured performance, the C-300 was the fastest car on the road in 1955. Only the Cadillac Eldorado came close. That car's V-8 generated 270 horsepower, but it weighed 1,000 pounds more than the C-300. This left the C-300 in a class of one. Packard had introduced an OHV V-8 for 1955 that pumped out 275 horsepower, but Packard was in such dire financial straits that its quality control processes were in the toilet, and the few cars it did sell for the 1955 model year all had to be repaired

BELOW: Bob Rodger and his team developed a reliable camshaft that made it feasible to use the Hemi in a production car.

OPPOSITE TOP: Rodger tasked Ed Quinn with creating a sporty car worthy of the Hemi engine for the 1955 model year—hence, the C-300.

OPPOSITE BOTTOM: Carl Kiekhaefer examines one of his Hemi-powered NASCAR racers in 1956.

FOLLOWING PAGES: A Carl Kiekhaefer Hemi-powered C-300 driven by Tim Flock won the NASCAR race at Daytona Beach in 1956.

before they were even sold to the public. Packard couldn't be considered serious competition, 275 horsepower or not.

As was often the case, Tom McCahill, the iconic automotive editor for *Mechanix Illustrated*, best described the phenomenal new Chrysler:

Here is the most powerful sedan in the world, and the fastest, teamed up with a rock-crushing suspension and a competition engine capable of yanking Bob Fulton's steamboat *over* the George Washington Bridge . . . This is definitely not the car for Henrietta Blushbottom, your maiden schoolmarm aunt, to use for hustling up popsicles. In fact, the 300 is not a car for the typical puddling male to use. This is a hardboiled, magnificent piece of semi-competition transportation, built for the real automotive connoisseur . . . On the beach I made a number of hard cuts and full, fast, 360-degree turns and found that there just wasn't the slightest bit of "plow" in this rig. It was as solid as Grant's Tomb and 130 times as fast . . . I also realize that the guy who buys this for his one-and-only family hack has rocks in his head. It's too masculine for a pet.

The major change to the front of the 1956 Chrysler 300 was the insertion of the letter "B" in the checkered flag on the emblem.

While a lot of people might have had enough rocks in their heads to tolerate the C-300's hard-edged sporting character, few could afford its exorbitant $4,110 price tag. A radio, heater, and power steering added an additional $295.50, and buyers could order extras such as power windows, power seats, a clock, and tinted-glass windows, further inflating the price. (Air conditioning was one of the few options not available.) Given the kind of commitment required to own "the most powerful sedan in the world," quite a few buyers stepped up to the plate. Chrysler sold 1,692 C-300s and exported an additional 33 cars (including one bare chassis) to other markets.

Virgil Exner's 1955 restyling of the Chrysler line proved an unqualified success. Sales increased 75 percent over 1954; basking beneath the halo of the mighty C-300 muscle car, Chrysler sold 176,039 of its 1955-model automobiles, and Chrysler Corporation as a whole had its most profitable year up to then.

Not only did Chrysler's powerful new performance cars sell in record numbers, they also cleaned up in NASCAR Grand National racing. Because the rules of the time ensured that the cars competing in the Grand National series really were lightly modified street cars rather than purpose-built race cars, a car like the C-300 that was significantly more powerful than the competition would kick everyone else's collective butt on the track. And that's exactly what happened, much to Bill France's consternation. If one car dominates the competition, the racing is much less interesting to watch than if the cars are more evenly matched. When the 300 began to win nearly every race, fans began to lose interest, and race attendance dropped.

TOTAL DOMINATION

In 1955 Carl Kiekhaefer, the owner of Mercury Marine, put together a racing team to campaign C-300s that included 1952 Grand National champion Tim Flock. Flock won the race at Daytona, and Lee Petty, who was also driving a C-300, took second. Flock and his C-300 dominated the rest of the season, winning seventeen more races that year and walking away with another Grand National championship. In all, C-300s accounted for a total of twenty-seven NASCAR wins that season.

In 1956, Kiekhaefer hired even more driving talent, signing Buck Baker, Herb Thomas, and Frank "Rebel" Mundy to campaign his carefully prepared 300Bs (as that year's models were known). Kiekhaefer's drivers won twenty-two Grand National races, Hemi-powered cars won thirty-three of that year's fifty NASCAR races, and Kiekhaefer had himself another Grand National trophy.

But he didn't get positive publicity for Mercury Marine, which had been the point of the exercise. The Hemis were so dominant that fans began to think of them as schoolyard bullies, to the point that they threw bottles at Kiekhaefer's drivers. Bill France and company weren't much more receptive, harassing the team with tech inspections, trying to find some

Don "Big Daddy" Garlits was the first drag racer to tap the potential of the Hemi design.

minor rules violations in an attempt to level the playing field. Of course, they found nothing— the Hemi was so much more powerful than any other engine on the track that there was no reason for Kiekhaefer to cheat.

But the Hemi's first period of total domination ended the following year, when Ford and GM introduced new engines that could better compete with Chrysler's beast. Kiekhaefer's well-funded Mercury Outboard team soon disbanded.

For the 1956 model year, Exner introduced his first tailfins. In 1948 Cadillac had introduced this design feature, which would come to symbolize American excess. Chrysler was coming relatively late to the tailfin game. Compared to the increasingly outrageous designs of its competitors, its fins were relatively

subdued and tasteful. Exner's mildly finned rear fenders blended perfectly with the longer and lower designs he created in the 1956 models by extending bodywork and bumpers.

The Hemi received a slight bore increase to 3.94 inches, resulting in a displacement of 354 cubic inches. Thanks to the overbore and a bump in compression to 9.0:1, power output of the base two-barrel Hemi rose to 280 horsepower.

THE 300B

Exner's modest first-generation tailfins looked nothing short of stunning on Chrysler's sleek 1956 300, now called the 300B. Chrysler made its revolutionary recirculating air-conditioning system available as an option on this model (an expensive option, adding $567 to the bottom line of what was already one of the most expensive cars sold in America) along with power seats, steering, brakes—the list goes on. Chrysler even partnered with RCA to offer an accessory it called "Highway Hi-Fi." This consisted of a built-in turntable that played special records and broadcast the sound through the car's radio speakers. A car

To make the optional turntable functional in a moving DeSoto required an extremely heavy arm to keep the record from skipping—something that didn't lend itself to extended vinyl life.

bouncing down the highway is a poor platform upon which to mount a turntable, and the idea didn't catch on, but kudos to Chrysler for recognizing the need for quality audio equipment at that early date.

The 300B was certainly the fastest car built in America. The base engine, a dual-quad 354-cubic-inch Hemi with 9.0:1 compression, pumped out 340 horsepower. When equipped with optional 10.0:1 compression pistons, output jumped to 355 horsepower. This was enough to propel the car to 140 miles per hour, making it fast even by today's standards.

The C-300 had been offered with a two-speed PowerFlite automatic transmission as standard equipment. In the 300B, this transmission was operated by system of dash-mounted buttons, rather than the column-mounted stalk used the previous year. This innovation would remain a Chrysler staple for almost a decade.

In response to the demands of customers who raced their 300s, Chrysler offered an optional column-shifted three-speed manual transmission. The C-300 had built a reputation as a performance icon both on the street and on the track, and Chrysler wanted to maintain that momentum. As a result, a buyer could order final drive ratios all the way up to a tractorlike 6.17:1.

DeSoto called its version of the Hemi the "Fireflite Eight."

LIVING LIFE A QUARTER MILE AT A TIME

In 1956 Chrysler set its sights on the one remaining form of American racing that was still dominated by flathead V-8s: drag racing. Drag racers had stuck with the inefficient side-valve design for the practical reasons of cost and aftermarket support.

As spectacular a car as the 300 was, it was still too expensive and too heavy for serious hot rodders. Overhead-valve V-8s might have completely taken over from their side-valve brethren when it came to the US passenger-car market, but there wasn't yet any speed equipment available for them. According to Don Garlits, who was by then a budding drag racer in Florida, OHV V-8s had rev-limiting hydraulic lifters, and parts to remedy this weren't readily available on a nationwide basis. The C-300 had solid lifters, but with a price tag north of $4,000, it was beyond the financial reach of the average drag racer. In his book *Tales from the Drag Strip* (Sports Publishing, 2004, cowritten with Bill Stephens), Garlits writes, "I once made the stupid statement, 'Those overhead valve engines will never outrun these flatheads.'"

Still, Garlits found the powerful Hemi engines useful. In the mid-1950s he bought a 331-cubic-inch Hemi from a junkyard and mounted it in the Ford coupe he used to tow

DE SOTO

INDIANAPOLIS 500 MILE RACE, MAY 30, 1956

Official
PACE CAR

his dragster to the strip. Garlits needed a strong engine because, as he wrote, "If you were towing your dragster and got behind some farmer on his tractor while you were on your way to or from the track, you needed some real power to pull out and get around him."

One day Garlits broke the transmission in his dragster. Rather than going home without racing, he decided to see what the Hemi-powered Ford coupe could do on the drag strip. When he told his wife, Pat, what he had in mind, she responded, "You'd better not break it, because if you do, we won't have any way to get home."

Well, I decided to give it a try anyway. I eased it to the line, and with those old 8.20×15 treaded tires on it, I had to take it easy when I left and not break them loose. I got it right, and I went through the gears and shot down the track. Now, our flathead dragster had made a full pass with a time of about 12.5 seconds at 108 mph. That coupe ran a 14-flat at 114 mph! On the way home . . . I said to Pat, "Honey, the first guy to put one of those Chrysler Hemi engines in a dragster is going to be the guy to beat."

And she said, "Well, you'd better put one in your dragster right away!" [I] didn't need to be told twice. Almost as soon as we got back, I dropped that Hemi into the dragster and couldn't wait to go up to Brooksville to see what we had. The engine still had the original ignition and a battery, it had dual-quads, and it went out and ran 10.5 seconds at 128 mph! I tell you what, the drag racing world around here was set on its ear! That kind of performance had never been seen before. I mean, with the 12.5s we had been running, we were winning Top Eliminator!

Garlits found a frame from a 1931 Chevrolet—choosing that year "because the bodies had so much wood in them that they'd rot away and you'd have the frame left over"—and built the *Swamp Rat*, his first purpose-built Hemi-powered dragster. By 1957 he had his Hemi-powered cars running through the quarter mile at 170 miles per hour, at a time when the world record was 168.22 miles per hour.

De Soto
most powerful car in the medium-price field!

DE SOTO DIVISION, CHRYSLER CORPORATION

255 hp Why wait for 255 hp performance in next year's cars . . . you can get it *today* in the powerful new 1956 De Soto. Here's the car that's more spirited and agile in city driving . . . safer and more comfortable at super-highway speeds . . . and costs hundreds of dollars less than you think! You'll find some De Soto models actually cost far less than dolled-up versions of the low-price three!

Your De Soto dealer is out to top his sales records of last year, and he's ready to make the deals to do it. That's why he's able to give you a truly fabulous trade-in on a big, luxurious new De Soto. Before you put a dollar down on any car . . . see and drive *and price* the smart **'56 De Soto—the car for the super-highway age.**

Pace car for the 1956 Indianapolis speed classic, the new 255 hp De Soto Fireflite, will set a scorching pace for thirty-three of America's fastest racing cars on Memorial Day, May thirtieth!

DE SOTO OFFICIAL PACE CAR 1956 PIKES PEAK AUTO HILL CLIMB

Push-button control is the easiest way ever invented to drive or park a car. Positive mechanical control. Try it today!

High torque take-off. De Soto with its mighty 255 hp engine will give you the fastest take-off you ever experienced! It outpowers, outguns, outhandles every other car in the medium-price field!

De Soto dealers present **Groucho Marx** in "You Bet Your Life" on NBC radio and TV

When reports of Garlits's exploits reached drag racing's spiritual home in Southern California, the racers there scarcely believed them. They thought that the Florida tracks where Garlits raced must be using faulty clocks, but Hemi performance was about to get even more unbelievable. Garlits might not have earned a doctorate from the prestigious Chrysler Institute, but he possessed a natural engineering brilliance, and he instinctively understood how to tap the wealth of power hidden within Chrysler's amazing Hemi. With a little tweaking to the fuel-delivery system, Garlits pushed his dragster through the quarter mile at 176.4 miles per hour in 8.79 seconds. "The Californians could believe it if they wanted to," Garlits writes.

In 1958 Garlits met three of the fastest drag racers in California at a track in Houston, Texas, and proceeded to beat each one, making believers out of the California hot rodders. Soon the gospel of the Hemi would spread from coast to coast.

In addition to its advanced styling, the *Norseman* foreshadowed the future of Chrysler engineering with its non-Hemi overhead-valve V-8.

MORE MOPAR MUSCLE

Resourceful hot rodders weren't the only groups taking advantage of the phenomenal performance of Chrysler's Hemi. The corporation's DeSoto and Dodge divisions soon built their own Hemi-powered muscle cars.

DeSoto's answer to the 300 series was the Adventurer. Like the 300, it was a luxury vehicle, occupying the top rung of the DeSoto line; it even offered the unique Highway

Hi-Fi turntable as an option. And like the 300, the Adventurer featured DeSoto division's most highly tuned version of the Hemi engine; DeSoto engineers extracted 320 horsepower from the 341-cubic-inch dual quad V-8. An Adventurer paced the 1956 running of the Indianapolis 500.

Dodge division had introduced a sporting car in 1954, the Royal 500, beating the C-300 to the market by a year, but this was just a low-volume version of the division's Royal convertible with a special trim package commemorating the car's service as the pace car in the 1954 running of the Indianapolis 500. And it still featured the decidedly unsporting pre-Exner bodywork.

Instead of offering a purpose-built performance model like the 300 and Adventurer for 1956, Dodge offered a performance package that could be added as an option to any of the division's models. Called the D-500, this option package boasted a tuned version of the division's Red Ram Hemi (which now displaced 315 cubic inches and produced

The stylish *Norseman* would have been the star of the 1956 auto show circuit, had it arrived in the United States safely. Unfortunately, it sank on the *Andrea Doria*.

260 horsepower), mounted in a specially braced frame with heavy-duty suspension components. This option package quickly became a favorite with law-enforcement agencies across the country.

If a buyer wanted the ultimate performance Dodge, he or she ordered a Coronet with a manual transmission, then specified the D-500-1 option. This package substituted the stock Red Ram cam with a racing unit and mounted a pair of four-barrel carburetors to increase power to 295 horsepower.

When the Italian luxury liner *Andrea Doria* sank off the coast of Nantucket, Massachusetts, she took an irreplaceable piece of automotive history with her: Chrysler's *Norseman* concept car. Like the K-310, it had been built in Turin, Italy, by Exner's favorite design house, Carrozzeria Ghia.

The *Norseman* embodied Exner's most ambitious design ideas to date. It featured aluminum body panels mounted to a frame consisting of a pair of cantilevered steel arches that swung up and over the passenger compartment. The car took the hardtop concept a step further and removed the A-pillar around the windshield so that the top relied solely on the C-pillar around the rear window for all structural support. This design allowed Exner to install an electrically operated glass panel that covered the passenger compartment. The panel slid forward, leaving the rear seat open to the elements. Futuristic styling touches included concealed headlights (a feature that had briefly appeared on DeSoto models just before civilian auto production ended because of World War II) and concealed door handles. In many ways, this car presaged the 1966 Dodge Charger.

THE POLY V-8

In a move that foretold the impending doom of the Hemi, the *Norseman* "was powered by a special advanced Chrysler engine," according to a Chrysler's press release of July 26, 1956, the date of the *Andrea Doria*'s sinking. Instead of a mighty Hemi, Chrysler's records indicate the car was equipped with a 225-horsepower version of the 331-cubic-inch "poly" V-8.

Chrysler had introduced a smaller engine in 1955 that was much less expensive to produce than the complex Hemi. Chrysler called this engine the poly V-8 after the engine's twin-domed combustion-chamber design, which the company called "polyspherical." This design placed the intake and exhaust valves in line with each other, allowing engineers to use just one rocker arm per cylinder. Even though the poly engine lacked hemispherical heads, it was no slouch. In stock two-barrel form, the 1956 model produced 225 horsepower; when equipped with an optional "Power Pak" (a four-barrel carburetor and dual exhaust), the engine put out 250 horsepower, putting it dangerously close to Hemi territory. That the *Norseman* featured a poly rather than a Hemi V-8 didn't bode well for the long-term prospects of the expensive twin-rocker engine.

Chrysler Corporation sales decreased dramatically for 1956; in fact, the US auto industry as a whole contracted that year, to the tune of 2 million fewer units sold when compared to 1955. All the US automakers were hurting, and all were willing to try something radical to turn sales around. Radical is just what the automotive stylists gave the public. And so, 1957 would be remembered as the year tailfins went over the top.

Chrysler had Ghia, a coachbuilder based in Turin, Italy, build the *Norseman* show car.

Virgil Exner was more than willing to go the mega-fin route in his designs, and he arguably designed exaggerated tailfins better than any other designer. In *Chrysler & Imperial 1946–1975*, Langworth quotes Virgil Exner Jr.:

My father was a real staunch believer in fins. Like a lot of designers at the time, he was tremendously influenced by Italian designs—the Alfa BAT and the Cisitalia, for example. The idea of the fin was to get some poise to the rear of the cars, to get them off of the soft, rounded back-end look, to achieve lightness. To my dad, Italian design represented these characteristics, and [he] was good at achieving a sculptured effect, a very contemporary proportion.

The fins of the 1957 Chryslers even served a functional purpose—they had been designed in a wind tunnel to provide stability at speeds over 60 miles per hour. But as the decade wore on and manufacturers designed increasingly exaggerated tailfins, designers abandoned any pretext of functionality. Few people believed such claims anyway. It didn't matter; the buying public loved the new Jet Age look—at least initially.

No one doubted the functionality of another innovation Chrysler introduced for the 1957 model year: Torsion-Aire Ride, which was Chrysler's marketing name for its torsion-bar front suspension system. In theory these bars, which replaced traditional coil or leaf springs, absorbed forces generated by road irregularities more efficiently than the traditional designs. Torsion bars had long been used in European cars, and Packard had employed them in both the front and rear suspension systems on its 1955 models. (The Packard design even had a self-leveling system operated by electric motors.) Improved handling was the ostensible purpose of Chrysler's torsion-bar system, but its main functional advantage was that the system didn't occupy as much space as the tall coil-spring system and allowed Exner to design lower hoods. Plus the marketing name "Torsion-Aire Ride" gave Chrysler dealers another selling point—no small consideration in the tough auto market of 1957. The downside was that the bars tended to fail, causing the front suspension to sag.

The three-speed TorqueFlite automatic transmission, button-shifted as had been its two-speed predecessor, appeared in 1957. The new transmission was much better able to harness the power of the Hemi engine, which now had a horsepower rating almost as excessive as the height of the tailfins sprouting up all over Detroit.

Exner mounted his pronounced tailfins on the 300, now called the 300C. (The letter designation would remain a tradition throughout the car's lifespan, with each successive year advancing one letter up the alphabet.) He also gave the car a distinctive trapezoidal grille. For the first time, buyers could choose a convertible version of the 300, but the real news came from the engine bay. Once again Chrysler's engineers had taken the boring bar to the Hemi, reaming the bores out to 4 inches. Combined with a stroke that was increased to 3.9

inches, the Hemi now measured 392 cubic inches. The twin four-barrel version of the engine mounted in the 300C produced 375 horsepower.

In case 375 horsepower wasn't enough, Chrysler offered an optional engine and chassis package consisting of a full race cam, 10.0:1 compression pistons, manual steering, a manual transmission, a heavy-duty clutch, and a limited-slip differential. The end result was a 390-horsepower car capable of running 145 miles per hour or better. *Mechanix Illustrated*'s Tom McCahill called it "the most hairy-chested, fire-eating land bomb ever conceived in Detroit."

The tailfins resonated with the general public, and Chrysler Corporation had a spectacular year. DeSoto did its part to contribute to the corporate coffers, helped by the successful Adventurer, which sold almost double the number of units of the previous year. The engine now displaced 345 cubic inches and generated 345 horsepower. That might have been a bit less hairy than the "hairy-chested" 300C, but it was still a lot, and the Adventurer was quite a bit less expensive than the Chrysler muscle car. The DeSoto was not cheap, but a buyer could get an Adventurer coupe for $932 less than a similar 300C, and a convertible version cost a whopping $1,000 less than the convertible 300C.

Dodge still offered the D-500 package, which included a 325-cubic-inch Red Ram Hemi that, when equipped with optional dual-quad carburetors, cranked out 310 horsepower.

In 1956 Chrysler followed the C-300 with the 300B. Chrysler could have continued down the alphabet and introduced the 300A in 1957, but it reversed gears and brought out the 300C instead.

Plymouth also joined the fray, offering a sporty model of its own: the Fury. This stylish car featured an engine—the Fury V-8, a 318-cubic-inch poly V-8 with two four-barrel carburetors, a solid-lifter camshaft, and a 9.25:1 compression ratio—that generated 290 horsepower, nearly as much power as a Hemi for quite a bit less money. The Fury made Mopar muscle affordable for a much wider audience.

Because of the success of the 1957 models, Chrysler made very few changes for 1958. Like all manufacturers of the time, the company felt compelled to make at least minor trim changes for the new model year, so designers made haphazard tweaks here and there, compromising the purity of Exner's 1957 designs.

The most obvious change to the 300 muscle car was that it changed from the 300C to the 300D. Engineers increased the compression ratio of all Hemi engines to 10.0:1 and installed a different cam in the twin-quad 300D engine, translating to 380 horsepower in the base model. This was up 5 horsepower from the previous year, but in exchange torque fell by 15 pound-feet, from 450 to 435. However, this was more than enough to propel a stock 300D through the quarter mile in 16 seconds flat at 84 miles per hour, and Norm Thatcher set a Class E record at Bonneville in 1958, getting his 300D up to 156.387 miles per hour. The last of the original Hemi muscle cars was a serious piece of equipment, and Chrysler's owner's manual issued a warning that owners should "have respect for its power and control its power with care."

The most intriguing option offered on the 1958 300D was the Electrojection electronic fuel-injection system. This ambitious system, developed in conjunction with Bendix Corporation, relied on complicated pretransistorized electronics that included an electronic modulator and fuel pump and required the mounting of a 40-amp generator. This $640 option

In 1958 the 300D featured wedge-shaped combustion chambers instead of the omnipotent Hemi design, as did all Chrysler products, signaling the end of the first Hemi-powered era.

increased engine output by 10 horsepower; in other words, it equaled the optional engine and chassis package of the previous year.

Or at least it would have, had it worked. In this case, the reach of Chrysler's vaunted engineers exceeded their collective grasp. Vacuum tubes are not well suited for life in the harsh environment of an engine compartment, and the Electrojection system proved a dismal failure. Chrysler sold just sixteen of the 300Ds equipped with the expensive system and ended up recalling all sixteen cars and retrofitting them with dual four-barrel carburetors.

END OF THE ROAD

Chrysler Corporation had already begun phasing out the Hemi in 1958; Dodge, Plymouth, and DeSoto performance models had begun using a new OHV V-8 design with a wedge-shaped combustion chamber, leaving just the 300D flagship with a Hemi engine.

By 1958 Chrysler had very little motivation to keep building the expensive Hemi engine. Racing success—the Hemi's raison d'être since Tommy Thompson had given the Hemi its first NASCAR victory in the Motor City 250—no longer mattered. The expense of building this complicated and advanced engine had been justified in part by the promotional value of having Chrysler products win races around the country. But in 1957, Chrysler, along with all other US automakers, abandoned the racetrack as a promotional venue.

As cars became more powerful and racing became more popular, people without driving talent began to emulate the exploits of their racing heroes on public streets. In many cases, these amateur "racers" competed in automobiles that were far too powerful for their skill levels. The results were spectacular wrecks worthy of inclusion in the goriest driver's-education films. Voters hell-bent on saving the country's hot rodders from themselves began complaining about fast cars, street racing, and accidents, prompting the federal government to start grumbling

When equipped with a 10.0:1 compression ratio, the 392-ci Hemi in the 1957 300C cranked out 390 horsepower.

about regulating the auto industry. In a preemptive measure, the Automobile Manufacturers Association (AMA), at the time the primary lobbying group for American auto manufacturers, instituted a voluntary ban on factory involvement in racing. Stripped of its promotional value, the expensive Hemi engine became virtually impossible to justify.

With the failure of the Electrojection system, Chrysler's mighty engine ended production on a somewhat low note. The carbureted versions were still the most powerful engines on the road—they wouldn't be surpassed in output for quite a few years to come—but they didn't dominate by the same margins as they had a few years earlier. Advanced engines from other manufacturers, and even from within Chrysler itself, were eliminating the need for building the complicated Hemi. After the 1958 model year, Chrysler stopped offering Hemi engines. It seemed highly unlikely anyone would ever resurrect the design.

The 300C featured one of the most luxurious interiors available in 1957, meaning it was also one of the most expensive cars on the market that year.

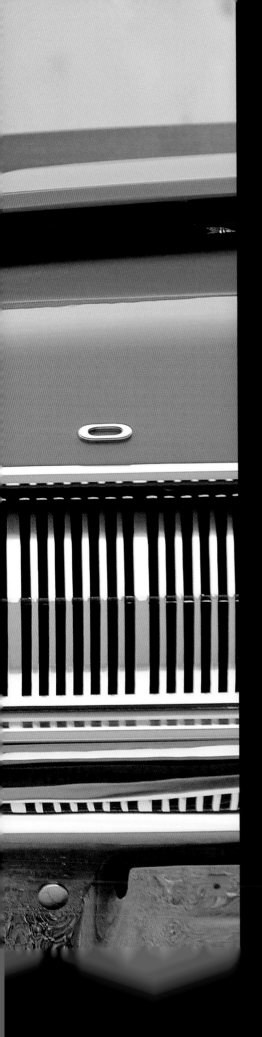

4

Hemi Resurrection

Chrysler engineers introduced the Hemi's replacement, the "wedge" B-block engine, in 1958, the last year of Hemi production. Because development money was too tight to design different engines for each division, as had been done with the Hemi, the company used this new engine across all divisions. To disguise the fact that the same mill powering a mighty Imperial also motivated a lowly Plymouth, each brand offered the new V-8 with slightly different displacements.

The new B engine would prove to be one of Chrysler's best and longest-lived engine designs. Distinguished by its deep-skirted block and front-mounted distributor, the powerplant earned the "wedge" nickname because its combustion chambers were wedge-shaped rather than hemispherical or polyspherical. Wedge technology more closely adhered to the orthodox thinking of the day.

Plymouth's highest-output version of the new engine, dubbed the Golden Commando by the division's marketing types, displaced 350 cubic inches and generated 305 horsepower. The top Dodge B-block

OPPOSITE: To save weight, the 1964 Dodge Hemi-powered race cars had their inboard headlights removed. Rather than shape new grilles, Chrysler extended

displaced 361 cubic inches and produced 320 horsepower when topped by a pair of four-barrel carbs; the DeSoto version cranked out 345 horsepower from its 361 cubic inches of displacement.

Chrysler offered the star-crossed Bendix Electrojection electronic fuel injection system as an option on the B-block engine for 1958. With this system, the Plymouth version produced 315 horsepower, the Dodge version produced 333 horsepower, and the DeSoto produced 355 horsepower, but as with the Hemi, B-block fuel injection was an unmitigated disaster. All were recalled and replaced with dual four-barrel carburetors.

In 1959 Chrysler replaced the Hemi engine in the 300E with a 413-cubic-inch version of the new wedge-head. Because the larger members of the B-block family gained their extra displacement in part through increased strokes, Chrysler dubbed the engine family the RB series, standing for "raised block." Engineers tweaked the RB engine in the 300E to produce 380 horsepower, the same as the base version of the Hemi had the previous year, but sales fell to their lowest level yet, and Chrysler sold fewer than 700 300Es. This was in part because of quality-control problems that Chrysler's cars had been suffering since the 1957 redesign, but the deletion of the infamous Hemi from the engine bay also contributed

to the car's failure in the marketplace. The new RB was a terrific engine, but it just didn't have the cachet of the Hemi.

In a classic example of bad timing, the Hemi was just coming into prominence at the drag strip when Chrysler discontinued the engine. Racers were starting to understand how to tap the Hemi's potential. When they first began using Hemis in their drag cars, they modified the engines in much the same ways they had modified their flatheads. They hadn't yet grasped the advantages of the Hemi's short stroke, a product of its oversquare bore and stroke ratio. As they had done with the flathead, they increased the stroke of the Hemi by building what they called "welded strokers," that is, by welding up extended-stroke crankshafts. In addition to lowering the engine's rev limit, the welded crankshafts often broke in competition. "At the time we didn't know diddly about crankshafts," Don Garlits admits in his autobiography.

When Garlits's stroker engine grenaded at a race in Biloxi, Mississippi, he made a discovery that would prove a major breakthrough in the sport of drag racing. In his autobiography, he recalls:

I had no idea that a stock 392 Hemi would run that fast, because up until then we were used to running strokers. Because we couldn't afford to get another stroker motor, I did the only thing I could do. I got a stock 392-cubic-inch Hemi and put forged racing pistons in it with aluminum rods. Man, if that engine didn't have that car running like a rocket ship! It was a short stroke, so it picked up the boost, and it was a more efficient engine. We never ran a stroker again.

BACKDOOR MEN

The most basic thing to understand about racing is that no one cheats; rather, every successful racer uses his or her resourcefulness to find ways to circumvent any and every rule that gets between him or her and victory. This has been the case since the first Mesolithic Nubian got in his occipital bun the notion that if he ran faster than the other Mesolithic Nubians, he could avoid becoming a Neanderthal sacrifice.

Just as racers and race teams find resourceful ways to circumvent racing rules, so too did manufacturers find ways to circumvent the AMA racing ban almost from the moment it was instituted. Short of fielding factory race teams, the easiest way for the manufacturers to capitalize on the promotional benefits of racing was to provide top racers with under-the-table support. Don Garlits was one of the earliest recipients of such backdoor sponsorship.

In 1958 the first full year of the racing ban, Garlits experimented with dragsters powered by Buick and Chevy engines. The folks at Chrysler had been following his on-track exploits and weren't thrilled to see him winning races in dragsters powered by its competitor's small-block engines. Garlits writes:

One day I got a call from Chrysler. Now, this was 1958. I had no relationship whatsoever with Chrysler. I was buying my engines in the junkyard. This fellow from Chrysler says, "We understand you ran a Chevy in your dragster."

I said, "Well, yes, I did."

He says, "Well, we don't like that. What's wrong with the Chrysler?"

I said, "It's something we do. Ya know, we're always experimenting with different things to see what we can develop."

And he says to me, "We'd be more comfortable if you'd take that Chevy engine out and put a Hemi back in the car."

I said, "Well, I had a Buick in there before."

"But you can drop a Hemi in there, can't you?"

"Yeah," I said, "I can do that."

He finally says, "Then we'd be happy to supply you with some engines if you can do that."

Now, here's what they did from then on. There were a lot of these wealthy guys who bought Chrysler 300s and ran 'em hard and put 'em away wet. These were good customers of Chrysler, and the engines were under guarantee. These owners would beat these cars until something broke, like a rod bearing or something like that, and they'd drive them back to the dealer and shout, "Hey, my engine blew up!" Chrysler would drop a nice new engine—a new short-block assembly—into their cars, make them happy, and send the old engines to me. It was perfect for me, because we had to grind the cranks anyway, and the engines were in pretty good shape otherwise. So after that, I got all of the 392 Hemis I ever wanted from Chrysler.

LEFT: Though down on power from their Hemi-powered predecessors, the Dodge Red Ram engines could still spin skinny bias-ply tires.

BELOW: When topped by a pair of Carter four-barrels, the 383-ci engine in the Dodge D-500 produced 320 horsepower.

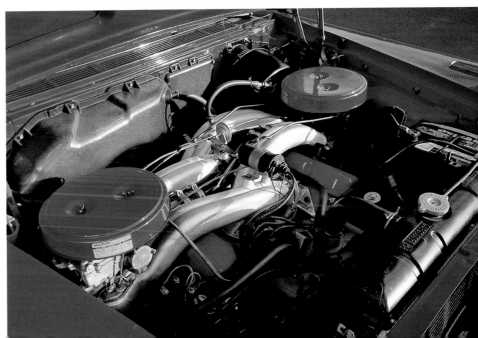

With backdoor racing sponsorship, the needs of the competition driver once again began driving Chrysler engineers to improve the corporation's engines. Racing drove the development of other manufacturers too, AMA ban or not, and Chrysler needed to develop stronger engines to beat the competition in the marketplace as much as at the track.

There are other routes to improved performance besides bigger, stronger engines. One is to build lighter cars, and for the 1960 model year Chrysler introduced an innovation that allowed engineers to shed massive weight from the company's production cars: unit-body construction. Unit-body construction combines an integrated frame and body, instead of placing a separate body on top of a heavy, ladder-type frame. Chrysler wasn't the first automaker to use this method of construction; the Italian automaker Lancia first used the technology in 1922, and a handful of US automakers, including Nash and Ford, had used it on some of their smaller cars. But Chrysler was the first automaker to build full-size unit-body cars.

MAXIMUM WEDGE

With lighter unit-body cars in its lineup, Chrysler had unknowingly developed one half of the muscle-car formula. The other half would be to develop a killer engine. Lynn Townsend, who took over as president of Chrysler Corporation in 1961 after the board of directors ousted Tex Colbert, understood the relationship between racing success and sales success. Townsend had two teenage sons who were heavily involved in Detroit's street-racing scene, which was centered around North Woodward Avenue. Their tales of hot Pontiacs beating Chryslers in impromptu drag races didn't sit well with Townsend. In late 1961 he ordered his engineers to develop an engine package that would make Chrysler cars the kings of the quarter mile once again.

Since the Hemi was officially dead, this meant developing a hot rod version of the RB wedge engine. This engine—officially called the Ramcharger when mounted in the Dodge chassis and the Golden Commando when mounted in the Plymouth, but unofficially called the "Max Wedge"—featured radical solid-lifter camshafts, large-port heads, and dual Carter AFB carburetors mounted atop a short-ram intake manifold. In its most powerful form, this engine package produced 420 horsepower, making the new lightweight Chrysler products the belles of the drag-strip ball. Pontiac had dominated drag racing in 1960. In 1961, Chevy's hot 409 had been the car to beat. In 1962, Mopars once again became the force to be reckoned with,

LEFT: The 413-ci Max Wedge engine was really a racing motor barely usable on the street.

BELOW: Virgil Exner's designs had grown downright goofy-looking by 1962, but the cars still ruled at America's dragstrips.

TOP: Plymouth paid a fair amount of attention to interior styling. This is one of thirteen 426 Max Wedge Sport Furys recognized by the Chrysler registry.

ABOVE: Dodge called its version of the Max Wedge the "Ramcharger 426," while Plymouth went with "Super Stock 426" for its version.

OPPOSITE: In the years between the last original Hemi and the design's rebirth in the mid-1960s, Chrysler didn't rest on its laurels. The 1963 Plymouth Sport Fury with a 426 Max Wedge engine would likely have been the fastest car at any local dragstrip.

and they would remain so for a very long time. Chrysler turned to Don Garlits to promote its hot new Max Wedge. In his autobiography, Garlits recalls his first experience with Chrysler's new drag-racing weapon:

> In the fall of 1961, Chrysler had me come up to Detroit and showed me the 1962 Super Stock Dodge. They said they wanted me to have one. It had a 413 wedge-head engine and a cross-ram intake manifold—it was a trick car . . . I took delivery of that car and it had a 3.31 rear axle in it. The first big race where all of the Super Stocks would be showing up was going to be at Green Valley, Texas. So my wife and I packed up our suitcases, threw them in the Dodge, and drove it to Green Valley! When we got to Texas, we went to a Dodge dealer and told them [to] put a 4.56 rear end in it. We drove it to the race, ran it, came back to the dealer, and had them put the 3.31 back in it. We drove all the way home to Tampa. It was really a stock car! And it was a fast car! It ran 13.5 or 13.6 at 112 miles per hour.

OPPOSITE: When topped off by a pair of Carter AFB-3447SA four-barrel carburetors pumping into combustion chambers with an 11.0:1 compression ratio, the Max Wedge cranked out 415 horsepower and 480 lb-ft of torque.

BELOW: This car came with a three-speed manual transmission but was upgraded to a four-speed in 1964.

FOLLOWING PAGES: This Sport Fury was one of three black Plymouths campaigned by Fenner Tubbs in Super Stock drag racing in 1963.

On his drive to Texas, Garlits couldn't resist having a little fun with the Dodge. While he and Pat were cruising down the freeway at 80 miles per hour, a hot-rod Ford pulled up beside them. The driver of the Ford had no idea what Garlits was driving; up to that point, Chrysler had only built thirteen Max Wedge–powered cars, and only a few Chrysler insiders knew what they were. The hot rodder thought he was going to have some fun at the expense of some shmucks in a Dodge sedan. Garlits sped up to 90, and the Ford sped up to 90. Garlits sped up to 100, and the Ford sped up to 100. Garlits sped up to 120, and the Ford sped up to 120, which was extremely fast for a Ford. Garlits writes:

> I had the 3.31 gears, remember. The Ford was just about to run out of breath. The Dodge had those two big dual quads on a cross-ram, and when I stepped all the way down on it, I couldn't believe I had been only running about half throttle! When I put it to the wood, I looked in the mirror and saw two thick black tire marks on the highway behind me! With a 3.31 gear, that Dodge is leaving rubber at 120 miles per hour and we just drove away from that Ford. I bet that guy talks about that to this day to his grandchildren!

AN ELEPHANT IN A COCKFIGHT

Garlits dabbled with Max Wedge–powered Super Stocker cars but focused most of his attention on his Hemi-powered Top Fuel dragsters, a sensible choice, since his Hemi-powered Swamp Rats continued to set speed record after speed record. Besides, Chrysler would soon have another project for him: developing a brand-new Hemi engine for Top Fuel racing.

Eternally the number-three American automaker (except when the company had surpassed Ford for a brief period just after World War II), Chrysler was willing to do just about anything to increase its market share. And if racing success was the way to get it done, the company's then-current batch of hot-rod boys would do everything in their power to ensure racing success—even if it meant bringing an elephant to a cockfight. That elephant took the form of a reborn Hemi.

It wasn't that the Max Wedge was underpowered. In fact, the engine would continue to dominate America's drag strips for some time. The Max Wedge had been bored out to 426 cubic inches for 1963, just slipping under the National Hot Rod Association (NHRA) limit of 427.2 cubic inches for Super Stock engines. Its parts list summarized the state of pushrod V-8 engineering art: double-row timing chain, one-piece short-ram aluminum intake manifold topped by a pair of four-barrel carburetors, header-type exhaust manifold, high-capacity fuel pump, dual-point distributor, forged-aluminum pistons, Magnafluxed connecting rods, high-strength valve-spring retainers, smaller crankshaft pulley (to limit belt speeds), and heavy-duty clutch with aluminum clutch housing. It even had a deep-sump oil pan that was baffled to prevent oil from sloshing away from the sump when the car inevitably wheeled off the starting line. With an optional 13.5:1 compression ratio, the engine produced 425 horsepower.

In order to transfer some of the Hemi's cachet to the Max Wedge, Chrysler tried to get top drag racers to abandon the Hemis and switch to the RB engines. Garlits remembers one such attempt:

Virtually all Hemi engines Chrysler built in 1964 were mounted in factory-built race cars.

In 1962, the NHRA must have had some clout with Dodge, because Frank Wylie called me up and he said, "We want you to build a gas dragster with the wedge motor and race it at the US Nationals. We don't want you to run the 392 because we don't make it anymore.

Garlits didn't have much luck with the wedge and switched back to the Hemi soon after. But his lack of success had more to do with his long-running feud with the NHRA than with any of the engine's deficiencies. Other racers had terrific success with the Max Wedge—at least, other drag racers did.

The problem was that the Max Wedge couldn't win on NASCAR's oval tracks. The engines performed well in short bursts, such as when being run flat-out on a quarter-mile drag strip, but the shape of the combustion chamber limited the size of intake and exhaust valves that Chrysler engineers could install. The wedge design also provided a less-than-optimum path for the fuel charge to enter the chamber and for exhaust gases to leave the chamber. While the wedge engine was a fantastic street engine and more than adequate for most forms of drag racing, these inherent design drawbacks resulted in diminished performance at the high rpm levels required for a successful NASCAR engine.

Lynn Townsend knew that to compete in an increasingly youth-oriented market, Chrysler would have to succeed in NASCAR as well as in drag racing. He sought advice from a group of engineers that included Tom Hoover, who was the engineering coordinator for Chrysler's race program at the time. Hoover, a Pennsylvania native who had grown up in a Mopar family—his father had worked in a Chrysler dealership—was also involved with the Ram Chargers, a group of Chrysler engineers who spent their spare time drag racing, both at the track and on Woodward Avenue. Hoover was a longtime fan of the Hemi engine, and his personal ride was a 1959 Plymouth into which he'd transplanted a 392 Hemi. In an August 2005 interview in *Hot Rod* magazine, Hoover recalls getting the approval to develop a new Hemi:

After the 1963 Daytona 500, won by Pontiacs, Mr. Townsend passed down the word: "What would it take to beat them and win the 1964 Daytona 500?" In response, the engineering vice president, a man named Bob Rodger, called a group of four or five of us together and we told him the best thing would be to go with the design we had experienced the greatest power with, and that was the Hemi. The outcome of all that was that in April of 1963 we were given the green light to fit Hemi heads onto the wedge block. And we did, very successfully.

Thus, in April 1963 Hoover's team was given the mandate to develop an engine that could win one of the world's most prestigious automobile races—and they had less than ten months to get the job done. Such a schedule should have been impossible, but Hoover and his crew were exceptionally dedicated and resourceful. The A-864 Race Engine Program they embarked upon would prove to be one of the most extraordinary, ambitious, and successful engine development programs in the history of the US auto industry.

But the hot-rod boys in Chrysler engineering were one step ahead of Townsend. An advance engine design group headed by Bob Dent had already begun developing hemispherical heads for the Max Wedge. Frank Bialk, the lead designer of the advance engine group, had begun drawing up plans several weeks before getting the official green light. In the 426 Max Wedge block, Bialk and the rest of Dent's team had terrific raw material with which to work. The crankshaft-support structure of the old 392 Hemi had been a weak point of the design, and the deep-skirted RB engine had a much stronger crankshaft mounting design. "We could put unbelievable cylinder pressure on it and the crankshaft stays where it is supposed to be," Hoover told *Hot Rod*. "It doesn't get pushed out onto the street where you have to drive over it." To further strengthen the bottom end of the new engine, Bialk designed main bearing caps held in place by cross bolts that ran through the engine block. In this design, the engine block itself bears some of the tremendous loads to which the crankshaft would be subjected.

Early on, the team made the decision to retain the original Hemi's valve angle. This created challenges for the team when it came to developing a rocker-arm system. One

The Hemi-powered 1964 Plymouth Belvedere was never meant to be driven on the street.

developmental goal for the new Hemi heads was for the rocker arms to have no more rotational inertia than the system used in the smaller 392 Hemis. This lack of rotational inertia was what allowed racers like Garlits and Keith Black to reliably run their engines up to 7,500 rpm. If the two valves were equidistant, as on the original engine, the exhaust rocker arm would be so long that it would limit engine rpm.

It also presented a packaging problem. A head with such long rocker arms would not fit in the engine bay of the intended recipients of the new Hemi, the corporation's lightweight B-body cars. The engines wouldn't fit because of the method Chrysler used to assemble its unit-body cars. Chrysler dropped the bodies down over the engines during the assembly process, and if Hoover's team didn't narrow the rocker covers, the engine wouldn't fit between the fender wells.

Hoover's solution was to tilt the entire head inward, toward the intake manifold, simultaneously allowing the use of shorter exhaust rocker shafts while allowing the engine to fit in the B-body cars. This resulted in slicing off a small section of the hemispherical combustion chamber, meaning that the 426 Hemi has a combustion chamber that is not completely hemispherical, which is why some people refer to the 426 as a "semi-Hemi." While this slicing of the combustion chamber did result in an extremely slight loss in thermodynamic efficiency, this was more than compensated for by an increased redline. Any performance loss would remain in the realm of the theoretical, a matter of more importance to armchair commandos than it would be to anyone actually racing a Hemi-powered car.

Designing head bolts strong enough to handle the tremendous pressure produced in the hemispherical combustion chambers proved another challenge. The wedge design used a five-bolt head-bolt pattern, as opposed to the four-bolt pattern used on the original Hemis. The problem was that when the heads were tilted inboard, there was no room for the extra bolt. Bialk's solution was to run the fifth bolt up from underneath the engine rather than down through the head itself. This system

In 1964 the only way to win at a dragstrip was to get your hands on one of Chrysler's new Hemi-powered cars.

would flummox many a dealer mechanic when a street version of the engine became available, but the engine was never designed to be driven on the street, much less worked on by some hack over at the local Dodge shop.

The team developed two separate intake systems: a dual-quad system for drag racing and a single-four-barrel system for stock-car racing. NASCAR regulations disallowed multiple carburetors, so the NASCAR manifold used a dual-plane design and featured a single Holley four-barrel carb. The drag-racing manifold used a cross-ram design in which the four-barrel Carter carbs fed the four cylinders on the opposite side of the engine. Knowing how much weight the complicated Hemi heads would add to the already-heavy 426 RB engine, Chrysler cast both manifolds from aluminum.

A MODEST 425 HORSEPOWER

No mass-produced engine before or since has ever been assembled from such high-end components as was the 426 Hemi. Forged rods connected the forged-aluminum pistons to the crankshaft, which was forged from either SAE 4340 high-strength alloy steel (for stock-car racing) or SAE 1046 carbon steel (for drag racing). The crankshafts were heat treated, machined, and shot-peened, then hardened through a nitride immersion process called Tufftride.

The team developed two camshaft profiles, one for drag racing and another for stock-car racing. Both versions worked against forged-steel mechanical lifters with brazed-on iron facing. These pushed heavy-duty steel-tubing pushrods against hardened forged-steel rocker shafts. The rockers featured full-length steel-backed bronze bushings and pressed-in hardened-steel inserts where they contacted the pushrods. The gigantic valves (2.25-inch intake and 1.94-inch exhaust) required two springs apiece to operate properly. The exhaust valves opened into 2-inch tubular-steel headers.

As soon as the Hemi head and block designs were finalized, Chrysler's foundry in Indianapolis began casting the engine blocks. Chrysler contracted the Campbell, Wyant, and Cannon Foundry Company of Muskogee, Michigan, to begin casting the cylinder heads. Once the cylinder blocks and heads were cast at their respective foundries, they were shipped to Chrysler's Trenton, Michigan, engine plant for machining. From there the early race engines were shipped to Chrysler's engine labs in Highland Park, where engineers would assemble them by hand. (When the street Hemi came out, final assembly took place at Chrysler's engine assembly plant in Marysville, Michigan.) Engineers in the Highland Park lab checked for cracks in the aluminum pistons and steel blocks, cranks, rods, and heads.

The entire assembly process took about 80 hours per engine, most of which was consumed by testing the components to make sure they were within the specified tolerances. The first engine was assembled in the first week of December 1963, just two months before the tech inspection for the Daytona race.

Chrysler rated the new Hemi at 425 horsepower, the same rating given to its Max Wedge predecessor. Everyone assumed that the artificially low power rating was the result of an effort on Chrysler's part to mask the true potential of its radical new engine, but in reality it was the result of a much less nefarious cause. In his book *Hemi: History of the Chrysler V-8 Engine and Hemi-Powered Muscle Cars* (Motorbooks, 1991), author Anthony Young quotes Steve Baker, a Chrysler engineer who worked on assembling the Hemi engines in the Chrysler lab:

Richard Petty won his first Daytona 500 in a 1964 Plymouth powered by the new 426-ci Hemi. The new engine proved so dominant that NASCAR banned it, forcing Chrysler to develop a street version of the racing engine.

"At the time," Baker remembers, "[the engine assembly lab] had a 400-horsepower Amplidyne dynamometer. Well, we knew we had a hell of a lot more horsepower. There were several of us there—the operator, myself, and the department manager, Ev Moeller. So we slide-ruled the observed power. We got 400 horsepower around 4,800 rpm. There was a possibility that we were going to break the dyno. Moeller was in charge and said to go ahead. He would take responsibility so the operator wouldn't get into trouble for damaging equipment. As I remember, we got up to more than 425 horsepower the very first run we made with the engine—and the dyno didn't break. Everyone was pretty pleased with that.

The Hemi-powered 1964 Dodge Lightweight was a stripped-down racecar.

Even though everyone knew the engine produced far more than 425 horsepower, there wasn't time to get the equipment necessary to produce the true horsepower figures. Later field tests showed actual output to be closer to 565 horsepower, but the 425 number stuck with the Hemi throughout its production lifespan. It really didn't matter anyway—the Hemi was never designed to win in magazine spec-sheet contests; it was designed to win races at the track.

In the weeks remaining before the Daytona 500, the crew at the Highland Park lab worked insane hours to prepare the engines. They ran the dynamometers 24 hours a day, curing the problems that cropped up with the new engine—and there were quite a few problems to cure, the most serious involving engine failures caused by cracking in the right side of the block. On January 28, 1964, just days before the February 4 prerace inspection at Daytona, Willem L. Weertman, Chrysler's manager of engine design, flew to Indiana to try to solve the problem. Through trial and error, Weertman and his crew arrived at a process in which the freshly cast blocks were placed in a large furnace and reheated to 1,200 degrees Fahrenheit to relieve any internal stress within the metal. Then the temperature in the oven was slowly lowered before the block was removed from the furnace.

These new blocks were shipped straight to Trenton for machining, then to the Highland Park lab for assembly. Weertman and his crew had accomplished a superhuman feat in preparing a durable engine block in such a short time, but the blocks didn't leave the foundry until February 3, which meant Chrysler wasn't able to ship them to the race teams for installation and testing prior to the Daytona tech inspection and preliminary races. Instead they shipped engines with the faulty block design and hoped they would hold up until the more durable engines were ready.

Meanwhile, the development team mounted one of the new Hemis in a stock-car racing chassis and headed to the Goodyear track at San Angelo, Texas. The car hit 180 miles per hour its first time out. This presented a dilemma for Chrysler: Townsend wanted to win the 500, but no one wanted the company's cars to be so dominant that they attracted the attention of the NASCAR establishment. Chrysler eventually intended to produce enough examples of the new engine to homologate it for NASCAR racing, but there was no way that would be possible in the time frame specified by NASCAR. If the cars were too dominant, the other manufacturers would squawk, forcing NASCAR to declare that the Chrysler offerings illegal for competition.

So Chrysler's racing department ordered the drivers not to do any wide-open laps during testing. This was in part because drivers were still using the original flawed blocks, but also in part to keep NASCAR officials from scrutinizing the new engine too closely. Drivers were ordered to lap the track at around the same speed as the Fords, which was around 170 miles per hour. Mostly this sandbagging tactic worked, though a few drivers couldn't resist showing off the new engine's potential; Paul Goldsmith qualified with an average two-lap speed of 174.91 miles per hour, a new track record, and Lee Petty's son, a dark-haired young lad named Richard, qualified with an average speed of 174.418 miles per hour.

When the qualifying races began, the new Hemi-powered Chryslers broke track record after track record. They also broke a block or two, but the revised blocks were on their way and would make it to the race teams just in time for the February 23 race. Hemi-powered Mopars took all three spots on that year's Daytona 500 podium, with Richard Petty taking top honors.

Townsend was so thrilled with the results at Daytona that he wanted to develop an engine to race in the Indianapolis 500, but he cooled his jets after learning that it would cost approximately $7 million and even then, the chances of winning would be slim.

As could be expected from the Daytona results, Petty won the 1964 Grand National championship. Hemi-powered cars won twenty-six Grand National races that year, humiliating Chrysler's competition in the process. The inevitable result of this was that the cars attracted the unwanted attention that Chrysler's race managers had feared.

WOODWARD AVENUE PRODUCT PLANNING GARAGE

By getting Chrysler Corporation involved in racing in such an overt fashion, Townsend was flaunting the AMA racing ban and putting the company at risk of retribution. Chrysler needed to tone down its racing activities, so it moved its racing program to a site away from Highland Park. Chrysler's corporate headquarters did not provide the ideal environment for race development; the engine lab in Highland Park couldn't be commandeered indefinitely for race engine development, and it allowed for too much corporate interference. Tom Hoover found an abandoned Pontiac dealership on Woodward Avenue, and the racing department relocated there. This facility became the epicenter for the development of Hemi-powered race cars.

The Woodward Avenue product planning garage proved an ideal location because Chrysler's Ram Chargers intended to take the new engine drag racing. They could develop products and install them during the day, then go out and test them in Woodward Avenue street races in the evening.

In order to homologate the Hemi for NASCAR, Chrysler had to build a certain number of production cars with the engine, though what that actual number was seemed to be something along the lines of we'll-know-it-when-we-see-it. This ambiguity gave NASCAR tighter control over the on-track action. If the sanctioning body wanted a car to compete, then the manufacturer had built enough examples; if a car proved too dominant and detracted from the close racing that put asses in the bleachers, then that car may well not have been built in a large enough quantity.

Of course, the actual number of production cars Chrysler intended to build with Hemi engines was fairly concrete, if you define production cars as "street-legal passenger cars": zero. The engine had not been developed with the requirements of street-legal passenger cars in mind. Instead, Chrysler intended to build a number of engines and complete cars for drag-racing use only; in other words, it planned to build drag cars to homologate its stock cars. In a paper that he presented to the SAE in 1966, Weertman explained the plan:

Immediately following the introduction of the engine, a production run of several hundred drag racing engines and cars were planned to be built. The production of the several hundred drag engines would be completed by the end of the 1964 model year. Another production run of several hundred drag engines was made for the 1965 model year automobiles, with a considerable weight decrease for the engines obtained by use of aluminum and magnesium components.

The 1964 Hemi cars were not created on a factory assembly line but rather were shipped to Automotive Conversions, a company that manufactured ambulances and limousines. There they were converted to stock-looking drag-racing cars. The only visual clues as to

what madness lurked beneath their hoods were shovel-like hood scoops that funneled huge amounts of fresh air to the hungry pair of four-barrel carburetors feeding the engines.

The 1964 drag cars stretched any definition of "production car" beyond the breaking point. Standard equipment included a Sure-Grip limited slip differential housing 4.56:1 gears, though the car could be ordered with optional gear sets ranging from 2.93:1 to 5.38:1. A compression ratio of 12.5:1 ensured that owners couldn't pull up to their corner gas station and fill the tank with whatever octane happened to be available, but the cars were never meant to be driven anywhere near the corner gas station. The rear window was replaced with 0.08-inch tempered glass, and window winders were eliminated to save weight. Even the insulating backing on the carpet was eliminated in the name of saving weight. These cars were meant for racing use only, a fact made clear in Dodge's promotional literature:

> The Hemi-Charger engine [Dodge's initial name for the Hemi engines in its cars] is designed for use in supervised acceleration trials and other racing and performance competition. It is not recommended for everyday driving because of the compromise of all-around characteristics which must be made for this type of vehicle. In view of its intended use this vehicle is sold "As Is" and the provisions of Chrysler Corporation's manufacturer's passenger car warranty or any other warranty expressed or implied do not apply.

This Dodge Super Stock is the only actual street car built with a Hemi engine for the 1964 model year. The original buyer ordered a 426-ci Max Wedge, but since that engine had been discontinued, Chrysler substituted one of the new Hemi race engines.

The booklet went on to name the available racing components, a list that read like a manifesto of the state of drag-racing technology: aluminum fenders, hoods, dust shields, front bumpers, bumper-support brackets, and doors. Plexiglass was available to replace the glass in the doors and front vent windows. Even without the optional drag-racing equipment, with the right person behind the wheel, each of the 1964 Hemis that Chrysler unleashed on the public was capable of breaking into the 11-second quarter-mile bracket right out of the box. Suffice to say, these Dodges and Plymouths were some of the quickest cars ever produced.

Not every budding drag racer could buy the new Chrysler Hemis, either, which further stretched the definition of "passenger car." Rather, the Woodward Avenue race shop provided cars to carefully screened racers, drivers, and teams, i.e., people with the skills to handle the potent machines and proven performance records that ensured the maximum publicity for Chrysler. The shop gave cars to proven racers like Don Garlits, while most racers couldn't buy a Hemi for any amount of money.

While the number of 1964 Hemis that found their way to the street is so low as to be almost negative, a few resourceful enthusiasts figured out how to acquire examples of the mythical beasts. Lynn Ferguson, a casual drag racer from St. Johns, Michigan, was one such enthusiast. Tired of losing in his 1951 Ford six-cylinder, Ferguson saved up and ordered a car he knew would win races: a Super Stock Dodge 440 with

When set up for drag racing, the Hemi engine was capable of running through the quarter-mile in 10 seconds.

Uh-huh, it's a Plymouth all right.
You can tell by the blur.

a 426-cubic-inch Max Wedge in Stage III trim. After four months of waiting, he learned that Chrysler had ceased production of Max Wedge engines, but they would be replaced by another engine.

Six weeks later he plunked down $3,820.25 cash and found himself the proud owner of one of the rarest American performance cars ever built. Other than the upside-down shovel on the hood, one of the few clues to the car's true nature was a sticker inside the glove compartment that read: "Notice. This car is equipped with a 426 cu. in. engine (and other special equipment). This car is intended for use in supervised acceleration trials and is not for highway or general passenger car use."

As if the regular Hemi wasn't special enough, the madmen at the Woodward Avenue garage developed an even more special version for 1965. Chrysler dealers announced the coming of this new drag-racing package on November 11, 1964. The cars—a Plymouth Belvedere given the production code "R01" and a Dodge Coronet designated

With their altered wheelbases, the A/FX cars were the predecessors to the Funny Cars that soon replaced them.

The 1964 Hemi race cars needed those big hood scoops to feed a hungry pair of Carter four-barrel carburetors.

the "W01"—looked like any other Hemi Super Stock car, except that the inner headlights were deleted on the Dodge. (Since the Plymouth had only two headlights to start with, this modification was unnecessary on that car.)

While the cars looked stock, their looks deceived. Because the lightweight 1964 Hemis had been so dominant, the National Hot Rod Association (NHRA) outlawed the use of aluminum body parts and plexiglass windows for 1965. To get around this, Chrysler made the bodies of the cars from lightweight steel that was 40 percent thinner than the steel used on the standard production cars. While Chrysler hasn't officially admitted this, the perpetrators responsible have since admitted that the cars' body parts were acid-dipped to make them lighter.

But the thing that separated these 1965 cars from their 1964 counterparts more than anything was the Hemi engine. The 1965 powerplant, internally referred to as the A-990 Race Engine, featured a redesigned camshaft and a few other tweaks. But its main innovation was its use of lightweight materials. Bill Weertman and his crew of miscreants cast the cylinder heads for the A-990 from aluminum and used aluminum alloy for the water-pump housing, oil-pump housing and cover, water outlet, and alternator brackets. They used magnesium for the intake manifold, and replaced the Carter AFB carburetors with a pair of Holley four-barrel units.

The A-990-equipped cars came ready to race as delivered from the factory, and owners couldn't load them up with options like heaters, air conditioners, or radios. The only choice a buyer could make was whether to select an automatic or a four-speed manual transmission. The A-833 manual had become available as an option in 1964, marking the first time a Hemi had ever been available with a four-on-the-floor transmission. Previous choices had been either an automatic slushbox or a three-on-the-tree manual. For 1965, the A-833 resided inside an aluminum housing when it backed a Hemi engine, rather than the heavy steel housing featured in more pedestrian applications.

The A727B TorqueFlite transmission was a new option for 1965. The 727 would prove to be one of the best transmissions of the classic muscle-car era and would remain in production in its original form until the 1990s; modified versions would be produced for years after that. The TorqueFlite is still a favorite of hot rodders today because of its reliability and durability. The A727B, the heavy-duty version that backed a Hemi engine, was modified for manual shifting and the valve bodies were reversed, so that the shifting pattern was the opposite of what it was in normal use. This allows drag racers to slam through the gears without worrying about hitting neutral or, worse yet, reverse. The A727B differed from the proletariat 727 in that it featured five discs instead of four to better cope with the Hemi's unbelievable power output.

Sticker price for the W01, which was given the cumbersome marketing name "Coronet Hemi-Charger," was $4,717, and the sticker for the R01, called the "Belvedere Super Stock,"

In a weight-saving move, Chrysler used liftoff lightweight hoods rather than steel hoods with heavy hinges and springs.

was $4,671. It's hard to imagine what might have accounted for the $46 price discrepancy in these otherwise identical cars, other than the fact that Dodge was a more prestigious nameplate than Plymouth. As if that mattered on the racetrack . . .

NASCAR'S REVENGE

Chrysler built 101 examples of each of these cars, with the Plymouth's production run ending in late 1964 and Dodge's in early 1965. They were more widely available than had been the Hemis of the previous year—you no longer had to be a connected racer to buy a Hemi, though most of them still went to professional teams and drivers. Chrysler had to build at least 100 examples of each car to satisfy the NHRA's minimum requirement to make a car legal for the Super Stock class. The company also built the cars in an attempt to homologate the Hemi for NASCAR racing, but Bill France and company didn't buy it.

In 1964, Chrysler had gone over the top with the Hemi, building an engine that was so dominant that it threatened to turn the Grand National series into the Hemi cup. At the same time, Henry Ford II wanted to win a NASCAR championship every bit as much as did Lynn Townsend, and the Deuce did not take kindly to having the lowly Chryslers humiliate his Fords for an entire year. In retaliation, Ford developed the Cammer engine, a 427-cubic-inch powerplant with a camshaft perched above each cylinder head.

Chrysler responded with the A-925 engine program. It figured that if one overhead cam was good, two would be better, and the A-925 was a double-overhead-cam design. Not only that, it operated four valves per cylinder instead of two, technically making it a pent-roof design rather than a hemispherical design—but since it was a Chrysler, everyone still called

A cutaway drawing of Chrysler's second-generation Hemi engine.

it a Hemi. Chrysler built a prototype but never actually ran the engine. The purpose of the A-925 was intimidation. Bob Rarey, Chrysler's chief engine designer at the time, tells the story as quoted in Anthony Young's *Hemi*:

Ford went down to Daytona for 1965 with their racing engine [the Cammer] . . . which wasn't a hemi, exactly, but was darned near, I guess. They said they wanted to race *that* against us. Ronnie Householder went in to Bill France and said, "Hey, look fellows, if you run that Ford engine, we're running this engine." He takes the cover off it and shows the four-valve Hemi. This engine had a 16-branch manifold. It was unbelievable. France just said, "As of now, the Ford engine isn't running and neither is *that*."

If Householder had intended to scare Bill France, he succeeded too well. France banned more than just the A-925; he also banned the Hemi. NASCAR's banishment of Chrysler's engine from its superspeedways so angered the automaker that it pulled all factory NASCAR-racing support for the 1965 season. In its attempt to avoid turning the Grand National series into the Chrysler Cup, NASCAR had inadvertently turned it into the Ford Cup, since Ford was the only factory still actively competing in the series.

Chrysler's withdrawal from NASCAR competition forced drivers to find something else to do for an entire season. It also left the mad geniuses at the Woodward Avenue garage with far too much time on their hands. They needed to find some worthy activity with which they could occupy NASCAR types like Richard Petty, Cotton Owens, and David Pearson. By this time the A/Factory Experimental (A/FX) class had superseded the Super Stock class as the premiere drag-racing class. This new class (which would eventually morph into the funny-car classes) proved a fertile ground for the talents of Chrysler's racing engineers, tuners, and drivers.

For 1965 Ford planned to campaign Mustangs and Comets powered by the Cammer engine. The A/FX rules allowed wheelbases to be decreased by up to 2 percent to put more weight on the rear tires, allowing them to hook up better off the line, but Ford openly flaunted that rule, so the Woodward Avenue crew decided to follow suit. They took six W01 and five R01 cars and moved the axles forward 15 inches. To accomplish this, engineers removed a 15-inch section of the rear floor pan and moved the rear end forward. A 15-inch flat pan was riveted over the area previously occupied by the rear axle. The crew modified the rear fenders to move the wheel arches ahead to the new location of the wheels.

The original run of 426 Hemis weren't really finished when they left the factory because Chrysler knew that every single one would be finessed by a racing tuner.

To compensate, the front wheels were moved forward 10 inches. Engineers fabricated new front side members and removed the crossmember that supported the upper control arms and torsion-bar springs. They fabricated a new crossmember and mounted it at the very front of the car, right below and just behind the front bumper. Since this crossmember normally supported the Hemi engine, new motor mounts had to be devised. Moving the front-end assembly proved a much more complicated job than moving the rear assembly because it required fabricating longer steering rods and torsion springs. Almost every suspension component had to be hand-fabricated, and each was made from the strongest material at the shop's disposal.

Since lighter materials were allowed in the A/FX class, these cars used lightweight fiberglass for their radically scooped hoods, doors, deck lids, front bumpers, instrument panels, and front fenders (which had the wheel openings moved forward to the very front of the car). The rest of the body was acid-dipped to remove excess weight. These cars were shipped in body-in-white form—meaning they weren't painted, just dipped in a light coat of primer, and it was up to the racing teams that got the cars to paint them with their own racing livery. The problem was that the acid-dipping must have left a thin residue of acid on the bodies; this kept eating away at the paint and sheet metal over the entire lifespan of the cars, forcing teams to repaint their cars multiple times.

Amblewagon, an ambulance-building company in Troy, Michigan, handled final assembly of the cars. Some were ready for the start of the 1965 season, but not all of them, and cars trickled out of Amblewagon throughout the winter and into the early spring. These cars were shipped to a carefully selected group of top racers. Ronnie Sox, Tom Grove, Butch Leal, Forrest Pitcock, and Al Exstrand received the Plymouths; Dick Landy, Jim Thornton, Roger Lindamood, Bob Harrop, Dave Strickland, and Bud Faubel received the Dodges. In addition, Bill Flynn from New Haven, Connecticut, had his W01 converted to A/FX specifications, resulting in a total of twelve cars built (thirteen if you count a developmental mule car that also competed in 1965, but that car appears to have been dismantled after the 1965 Winternationals in Pomona, California).

The American Hot Rod Association's (AHRA) rules allowed these altered-wheelbase cars to compete in its Ultra Stock (U/S) class, but the NHRA took umbrage at Chrysler's flaunting of the organization's 2-percent rule regarding the relocation of the rear axle and banned the cars from its A/FX class. As a result, the Woodward Avenue garage built four cars to the same specifications as the altered-wheelbase cars, except that the axle was only moved ahead the allowed 2 percent. These are referred to as the "legal 2-percent cars."

Wherever the altered-wheelbase cars were allowed to compete, they dominated the competition and broke all existing records. On April 24, 1965, Ronnie Sox of the fabled Sox & Martin team ran a 9.98 quarter mile at the drag strip in York, Pennsylvania, a new record for a stock-bodied automobile without forced induction. Sox used a new Hilborn fuel-injection system developed by Chrysler's Woodward Avenue race team to set his record time.

We're big on volumetric efficiency.

That way, our engines stay out front. Along with our cars.

Take the Plymouth Belvedere Satellite above, with its high-performance Plymouth Commando 426 wedge-head V-8. That power plant is the street version of our competition-designed 426 Hemi engine, which holds more records than our competitors care to count.

The Plymouth Satellite's Commando 426 V-8 has high-performance valve springs, cam, pistons and plugs.

Hydraulic tappets, dual breaker distributor, nonsilenced air cleaner, dual exhausts, heavy-duty clutch. And 365 horsepower.

Choose: Satellite hardtop or Satellite convertible. Axles to your driving tastes. Standard engine: 273-cu.-in. V-8. Optional V-8's: The 318-, 361-, the 383-cubic-inchers. And, say we immodestly, the optional high-performance Plymouth Commando 426 V-8.

Standard on the Belvedere Satellite are front bucket seats, center console with glove box, Safety-Rim wheels, custom wheel covers with spinner hubs, torsion-bar suspension.

Volumetric efficiency. You can research that one further. Or you can just tool on down to where they're giving free Plymouth Satellite rides. That one's a little easier to find.

THE ROARING '65s
FURY
BELVEDERE
VALIANT
BARRACUDA

Plymouth

 PLYMOUTH DIVISION **CHRYSLER** MOTORS CORPORATION

5

The Street Hemi

In banning the Hemi from NASCAR's superspeedways, Bill France inadvertently spurred the development of the street Hemi. Chrysler still wanted to race in the Grand National series, and the only way that could happen was for the company to offer a version of its Hemi race engine as a regular production option in its passenger cars.

Right from the start of the A-864 Race Engine Program, Chrysler's engineers looked into means of reducing the staggering production costs of the Hemi in order to make the engine viable in a street-legal vehicle. There were no easy ways to avoid the expensive manufacturing costs while still producing an engine that was as reliable as it was powerful—if anything, developing a civilian version for the street would add to the astronomical costs of the engine program. Besides, Chrysler already had one of the most powerful regular production street engines available during 1964: its 365-horsepower, 426-cubic-inch RB.

OPPOSITE: The original 1966 Charger sort of had the styling that muscle car buyers sought, but the 1968 redesign nailed it squarely between the eyes.

The 1966 Belvedere
HP2 was one of the first
Plymouths to receive
the street Hemi as a
regular option.

Yet people still mythologized the mighty 390-horsepower Hemi from the previous decade. The engine had developed its own mystique, and the marketing folks at Chrysler wanted to capitalize on the halo effect a new Hemi would have across Chrysler's entire product line. On February 6, 1965, styling manager J. C. Guenther and head of engine development H. R. Steding each received a memo jointly written by Chrysler engineers Robert Cahill and Bob Rodger. This document, perhaps the most famous memo in the history of the US auto industry, had the rather dry title "Hemi Performance Option Super Stock and 'A' Stock Competition." It outlined the following directive:

Please release a hemispherical combustion chamber engine for "B" Series [referring to the company's midsize B-body cars, which were in the process of being redesigned for the 1966 model year] with the following general characteristics:

1. Intake manifold to have two four-barrel carburetors.
2. Cylinder block to maintain cross tie bolt main bearing caps.

3. Cast Iron exhaust manifold.

4. Solid lifters are acceptable but not preferred.

5. Pistons—forged are acceptable and thermally controlled preferred.

6. Manifolding and camshaft to be designed to give the best high-speed power possible while still maintaining a reasonably drivable vehicle for summer and winter.

7. Automatic and four-speed transmissions required (four-speed to have development priority).

8. No air conditioning required for "B" Series.

9. Limited warranty is acceptable for "B" Series usage . . .

This engine to replace eight-barrel wedge requested in Product Planning Letter . . . dated 8/5/64.

This became one of the most published memos ever because it announced the birth of the street Hemi. According to the memo, Chrysler expected to build 5,000 to 7,500 Hemi-equipped cars per year. In reality, the company sold fewer than half of the lowest

BELOW: In 1966 a Plymouth with a street Hemi hit 160 miles per hour on the Bonneville Salt Flats, setting a new class record.

FOLLOWING PAGES: NASCAR regulations forced Chrysler to introduce a street version of its Hemi race engine for the 1966 model year, including under the hood of this Belvedere II.

ABOVE: If Thomas Aquinas's brain melted down when he contemplated how many angels could dance on the head of a pin, it would have exploded like an overripe carbuncle if he'd considered how many angels could have a polka party on a Hemi valve cover.

RIGHT: Cramming that giant Hemi engine with its extraordinarily wide heads and valve covers under the hood of a street car required a bit of trickery.

production estimate for Hemi-powered B-bodies in 1966, which Rodger and Cahill probably expected all along. The inflated estimates likely reflected the need to pad sales projections in order to create a profit-and-loss estimate that would fly with Chrysler's board of directors. (Most P&L assessments don't include a field for "Halo Effect.")

The birth memo put the street Hemi, given the internal code A102, on a fast-track development program, thus ensuring it would hit the streets by year's end so that Chrysler's cars could qualify for the 1966 NASCAR season. The resulting street Hemi varied less from its racing sibling than one would expect, given the expense of building the race version, but that was in part the result of the accelerated development schedule. It would take four more years for Chrysler's engineers to develop a marginally civilized street Hemi.

The new-for-1966 Dodge Charger featured styling elements from the _Norseman_ concept car that sank with the _Andria Doria_ (see Chapter 3).

Compression ratio in the street engine dropped to a more reasonable 10.25:1, allowing the engine to run on the highest-grade pump gas then available. If an owner needed to refill the tank on a car equipped with a race Hemi, they needed to make a trip to the local airport or the nearest racetrack to get the fuel with the octane rating required by the car's 12.5:1 compression pistons.

In an attempt to make the Hemi more streetable, engineers used a camshaft with less lift and overlap. They lowered valve-spring rates to make the valvetrain more reliable at steady rpm, and also to lower the rev limit to bring power output down to the advertised 425 horsepower. They swapped the cross-ram intake manifold with an aluminum unit that mounted the two Carter four-barrel carburetors in a parallel line above the engine's

ABOVE: Plymouth's answer to the Dodge Charger was the Belvedere-based GTX introduced in 1967.

OPPOSITE: The 1968 GTX shed the Belvedere nametag and stodgy styling.

FOLLOWING PAGES: Ordering a Hemi engine over the stock 440 RB engine in a Plymouth GTX cost the buyer an extra $605—no small amount in 1968 dollars.

camshaft. Instead of the chrome valve covers used on the race engine, the street Hemi featured valve covers coated in a black crinkle finish. In a cost-saving move that would address one of the few weak links in the early race Hemis, Chrysler engineers replaced the tubular-steel headers of the race engine with cast-iron exhaust manifolds.

Other than these changes, the new street Hemi was pretty much identical to the race version. It used the same double-roller timing chain, the same rugged rocker-arm system, and the same optional heavy-duty A727B TorqueFlite automatic transmission. Chrysler built the street Hemi to near-race specifications because it knew that a good number of the cars—perhaps the majority—would end up seeing the noisy side of a drag strip. Since part of the reason for the car's existence was to provide a halo effect for the entire Chrysler lineup, the company needed the street Hemi to withstand the rigors of drag racing. Cars that broke in front of huge crowds of people on Sunday weren't likely to sell in huge numbers on Monday.

Chrysler's Marine and Industrial division in Marysville, Michigan, assembled the street Hemi, giving each engine almost the same amount of individual care and testing as Tom Hoover's team had given to the race engines built at the Highland Park lab. Even though the engines were rated at 425 horsepower, which was a pretty

ABOVE: When Chrysler
sold 44,599 examples of the
new-for-1968 Road Runner,
including 1,019 equipped
with Hemi engines,
the executives at rival
automakers took notice.

OPPOSITE TOP: Although
called a "street Hemi," the
426 Hemi was really much
better suited for streets no
longer than a quarter mile.

OPPOSITE BOTTOM:
The new Road Runner
proved a perfect platform
for Hemi power.

FOLLOWING PAGES: For
1968, Chrysler's B-body
muscle cars received
a desperately needed
redesign.

accurate figure for the detuned street Hemi, most buyers knew they were getting hand-built race engines that were just a few modifications away from being 500-plus-horsepower drag racers.

On January 29, 1965, Chrysler announced it would be making street versions of the Hemi available as optional engines for the company's 1966 B-body cars: the Plymouth Belvedere and Dodge Coronet. These were crisply styled cars that have aged well and are still extremely handsome today, but in 1966 they seemed a little conservative when compared to the muscle cars being built by General Motors and Ford Motor.

But Chrysler also offered a new B-body model for 1966 that was aimed squarely at the emerging muscle-car market: the upscale Dodge Charger. While the other B-body cars featured styling that wouldn't scare anyone's grandmother, the Charger had the sleek, sexy look a car needed to go up against the likes of the GTO and Malibu SS, thanks to its sculpted fastback roofline. The Charger had other styling touches that set it apart from the crowd, including headlights hidden behind doors in the grill and bucket seats not only in the front but in the back as well. Budget constraints kept much of the Coronet's sheet metal on the Charger, but no one would confuse the two. Visually, the Charger had enough unique content to distinguish it from Grandma's grocery-getter.

Dodge's response to the Road Runner was the Super Bee.

The Charger proved an ideal home for the street Hemi. If a buyer was rich enough and brave enough to spend the extra $1,105 needed to check the "Hemi" box on the option sheet, he or she had one of the fastest muscle cars built at the time. Even though it was heavy, at 4,390 pounds, a 1966 Charger with a street Hemi was good for a 14.16-second quarter mile. From there, an owner could improve the number dramatically by opening up the exhaust and mounting a set of sticky tires—the Hemi could spin the original-equipment Blue Streak street rubber down to the cords in short order.

Chrysler marketed the new Charger to the emerging baby boom market, a massive group of consumers who were driving the US auto market by 1966. Ad copy for the new Hemi-powered Charger attempted to capture the youth lexicon of the period (with limited success), making obvious references to Ford's popular Mustang: "Dodge Charger with a big, tough 426 Hemi up front makes other steeds look staid. Both for show and go. Charger looks beautiful standing still. And the optional Hemi V-8 supplies a kick to match, with 425 muscular horses. Not a pony or a kitten in the bunch. The hot setup? You bet."

Plymouth also introduced a more upscale B-body model for 1966: the Belvedere Satellite. Unlike the Charger, which had unique fastback bodywork, the Satellite was basically a

Belvedere with a tasteful chrome trim package. Fitting the massive 426 Hemi in the engine bay of Chrysler's B-body cars took more than a little ingenuity. The right front shock tower had to be modified to make room for the engine, and the booster cylinder for the brakes had to be moved. Even so, the cylinder had to be removed to adjust the valves, an all-too frequent occurrence. The brake cylinder had to be removed just to get access to the rearmost spark plug on the driver's side. No one ever accused a street Hemi of being user friendly.

The automotive press made a complete spectacle of its collective self attempting to find superlatives superlative enough to describe Chrysler's amazing new engine. In the October 1965 issue of *Hi-Performance Cars*, Martyn Schorr wrote: "This engine is without a doubt the hottest hunk of iron to hit the street in the last ten years." The following March, Schorr described driving 160 miles per hour in a Plymouth street Hemi in the pages of the magazine:

We made the trek in record time, occasionally opening up all eight barrels to prevent the high torque hemi from feeling neglected! The transition from two to four and then to eight barrels was smooth as silk and the hemi really didn't feel its oats until the tach needle soared past the 3,800 rpm mark. And we really mean soared!

The Charger proved a hit with buyers, and Chrysler sold 37,334 of them in 1966, though only 468 buyers—1.2 percent of all Charger customers that year—elected to equip their cars with the expensive Hemi engine. The other 98.8 percent drove off with the 325-horsepower

Plymouth managed to cram 70 Hemi engines in the bays of 1968 Barracudas destined only for dragstrips.

383-cubic-inch B-block. Occupying lower rung on the Chrysler engine ladder in 1966, the B-block made much more sense for the average driver. In his book *Muscle Car Confidential: Confessions of a Muscle Car Test Driver* (Motorbooks, 2007), author Joe Oldham describes his attitude toward the Hemi at the time: "The Hemi engine was better suited to full-throttle operation on a racetrack (after a blueprinting and supertuning) than to street use. The huge sewer-size ports and twin 4-barrel carbs made zero low-end torque and the solid lifters had to be adjusted every two miles." In addition to saving the buyer $1,000 when compared to the Hemi, the 383 Charger was as quick from 0 to 60 as the expensive Hemi, thanks to its 425 pound-feet of torque, which edged out the 420 pound-feet produced by the Hemi. Of course, by the quarter-mile point, the Hemi disappeared into the distance, leaving the 383 for dead, but in that era most performance contests in the United States took place over a distance of ¼ mile or less.

Likewise, buyers of the other B-body cars chose the Hemi in more limited quantities than predicted. Plymouth's new Belvedere Satellite sold well, with the division moving 38,158 examples, but just 530 of those had Hemi engines. Instead of the projected 5,000 to 7,500 units, Chrysler sold 2,428 Hemi-equipped B-bodies for the 1966 model year. For most people the Hemi was simply too much engine. Even those who could afford the steep asking price seldom had the skill to handle a car with that powerful an engine.

BELOW: Dodge built 80 A-body Dart Hemi racers.

OPPOSITE: The Charger's flying buttresses looked great, but they were aerodynamically awful, so Dodge built a small run of Charger 500 models with aerodynamic designs meant to make them more competitive in NASCAR.

FOLLOWING PAGES: In 1969 only ten buyers ordered Road Runner convertibles with Hemi engines, and this example is just one of four equipped with four-speed transmissions.

Regardless of whether or not they could drive the car, the few people who did check the Hemi box on the option sheet certainly got their money's worth in bragging rights; any discussion about who had the fastest car in town usually ended the instant someone said, "I've got a Hemi." The street Hemi might not have been the most popular choice for Charger power, but its very existence escalated the muscle-car performance wars raging in Detroit.

RACING DOMINATION

Quite a few of the Hemi cars did find homes with serious racers. Since Chrysler had focused its resources on developing the street Hemi, the company didn't offer a Super Stock or drag racing special for 1966. Instead, racers had to buy production cars and convert them to race spec themselves. Since the strongest and lightest available body style was the unlovely two-door post sedan, which had much less pleasing lines than the stylish (but less rigid and heavier) hardtops, it's a fair bet that many of the Hemi-powered two-door post cars sold in 1966 ended up competing at drag strips around the country. That equates to 83 Dodge Coronets and 136 Plymouth Belvederes.

To appeal to drag racers, Chrysler offered a series of optional deletes that both saved weight and reduced the purchase price. For example, if a buyer was savvy enough to order option code 416, he or she could have the heater and radio deleted, saving weight and

$70.32 in the process. After that, a buyer could rely on the burgeoning aftermarket to convert the car into a full-on drag racer.

When Chrysler made the Hemi a regular production option that was available in its passenger cars, NASCAR had no choice but to allow the it back on the superspeedways. In 1966 Richard Petty started the Daytona 500 from pole position and drove his Petty Enterprises–prepared Plymouth Satellite to victory. Petty led the race for 108 laps, and Paul Goldsmith, another Plymouth driver, led for another 43 laps before falling to the back of the pack because of mechanical difficulties.

In all, Hemi-powered Chryslers accounted for seven of the top ten spots in that year's race. David Pearson, who finished third in a Cotton Owens–prepared Dodge Charger, went on to win fifteen races that season, earning Dodge a Grand National championship. This was the most victories one driver had earned in a single season since Tim Flock had won eighteen races in one of Carl Kiekhaefer's C-300s in 1955. In all, Hemi-powered cars earned thirty-four victories in the 1966 Grand National series.

Chrysler dominance became even more complete in 1967. The Hemis got off to a rough start, getting beaten badly by the Holman-Moody Fords driven by Mario Andretti and Fred Lorenzen at Daytona, but Petty went on to earn twenty-seven Grand National wins, a record that stands to this day, and he easily clinched the 1967 Grand National championship.

The 1966 B-body cars sold well enough for Chrysler, though the model designed for the youth market—the Charger—failed to strike a chord with baby boomers. Compared to the 72,272 Chevelle SS 396s sold by Chevrolet, the 96,946 GTOs by Pontiac, and the breathtaking 607,568 Mustangs by Ford, the 37,344 Chargers that Dodge moved indicated the division's interpretation of a sporty car wasn't connecting with this demographic.

Though the Daytona Charger could be had with a wedge engine, a car this excessive deserved the most outrageous engine on the market.

For 1967, Chrysler offered a pair of new B-body models aimed squarely at the muscle-car market: the Dodge Coronet R/T, which stood for Road and Track, and the Plymouth GTX, which apparently stood for nothing in particular but sounded like a car that could kick a GTO's ass. These cars still featured the rather conservative bodywork of the 1966 models, but with their nonfunctional hood scoops—the R/T featured one centrally mounted scoop, a miniature faux version of the scoop from the Super Stock cars, and the GTX had a pair of fake scoops above the cylinder banks—they were a step in the right direction, something to attract buyers while Chrysler prepared radically restyled cars for the 1968 model year.

Each car could be ordered with an optional Hemi, which was little changed from the 1966 engine, but there was little need for change because the base engine in both cars was a new high-performance wedge design that offered better street performance than the Hemi. In 1966 Chrysler had introduced a 350-horsepower, 440-cubic-inch RB engine for its full-size luxury cars, the Imperial and New Yorker. When mounted in the sporty 1967 B-body muscle cars, the engine received a hot-rodding treatment consisting of special heads with 10 percent larger valves and stiffer valve springs, hotter camshafts, and a huge Carter AFB four-barrel carburetor.

ABOVE: In 1970 the price of the optional Hemi in a Charger had risen to $841.05.

LEFT: Bobby Isaac steers his Dodge through the high bank at Chrysler's test track. The only real reason Dodge built the Charger Daytona was to be more competitive in NASCAR. In the process they created the first 200-mile-per-hour supercar.

The 1970 Charger was beginning to look dated alongside the competition.

These tricks raised the horsepower rating to 375, the highest of any engine equipped with hydraulic lifters at the time.

But peak horsepower was not what this engine was all about. It was about torque, lots and lots of tire-smoking torque. The engine, called the 440 Magnum when mounted in a Dodge and the 440 Super Commando when mounted in a Plymouth, churned out a class-leading 480 pound-feet of torque. This meant that the base-model GTX or R/T would outrun the same car equipped with an optional (and expensive) Hemi in an impromptu stoplight drag, at least in stock form. Thus, not a lot of people went into debt to order a Hemi for cars that were going to live their lives on the street instead of on the track.

The year 1967 was not a good one for restraint, and Chrysler's B-bodies, with their restrained styling, suffered mightily. Charger sales fell to just 14,980 units, and sales of all three B-bodied muscle cars—the Charger, Coronet R/T, and GTX—totaled a mere 37,176 units, fewer than the Charger had sold alone the previous year. Hemi sales, too, declined precipitously; only 1,121 buyers found the fortitude to equip their B-body cars with the expensive Hemi engine in 1967, less than half the number sold in 1966. Apparently the new 440 was taking a hefty bite out of the Hemi's diminishing piece of the market pie.

While Chrysler dealers lamented the downturn in sales, Mopar drag-racing enthusiasts had something to cheer about in 1967: a special run of Hemi cars equipped with a drag-racing package. These were cars designed to compete in the NHRA's Super Stock/B class. In what seemed a contradictory move, Chrysler built these modified Belvederes (production code RO23) and Coronets (production code WO23) using two-door hardtop bodies rather than the lighter, stronger two-door post sedans. This was because hardtops were more popular than posts. Chrysler's primary motivation for building such cars was to drive traffic to Dodge and Plymouth showroom floors, so the race department decided that the competition cars should look like the street cars people actually wanted to buy.

Each of these cars was identically prepared, with white paint and black vinyl interior. The cars retained stock bodywork and didn't use any lightweight fiberglass or aluminum panels. The only outward clue to the true nature of the drag-package cars was the steel hood scoop needed to feed air into the gaping maw of the Carter carburetors.

Automatic-equipped cars came with an 8.75-inch Chrysler differential that housed 4.86:1 gears, and the four-speed manual cars came with a Dana 60 that housed 4.88:1 gears. The A-833 four-speed transmissions were modified to what Chrysler called "Slick-Shift" specification, in which the synchronizers were removed and every other tooth was machined off the engagement gears. This system really was slick for full-on clutchless power shifting, but it was lousy for street use. The engine was a standard A102 street Hemi with a modified intake manifold that used a pair of modified Carter carburetors.

The Dodge listed for $3,875 and the Plymouth for $3,831. Since no options were available (though a few buyers managed to add a small geegaw or three to the order sheet), these cars were identical to one another except for a slight crease here or there in the bodywork, so it's hard to see Chrysler's logic in pricing the Dodge $44 higher than the Plymouth. As had been the case in 1964 and 1965, the price of these drag specials didn't include a warranty, real or implied, and each car carried the now-familiar warning: "This model is intended for use in supervised acceleration trials and is not intended for highway or general passenger car use."

ROAD RUNNERS AND SUPER BEES

Up until this point, Chrysler had relied on its engineering prowess to compensate for its shortcomings in styling. As had been the case with the early pre–Virgil Exner Hemis, the public turned away from Chrysler's dated designs. This was a difficult fall from grace for a company that had become famous for the stylish cars that flowed from Exner's pen. Chrysler spent much of the 1960s trying to catch up with the competition when it came to auto styling. When the Charger hit the streets in 1966, it found itself a couple of

This is one of just two factory Hemi Challengers ever built with the fiberglass hood from the Challenger T/A Trans Am racer. It's the real deal: its fender tag lists option N94—the T/A hood. This was a special-order that the owner of Vissings Dodge in Jeffersonville, Indiana, let an employee request as a demo if he promised to buy the car within one year.

Only twelve customers checked the "Hemi" box when ordering convertible Challengers in 1970—nine in the United States and three in Canada.

years behind the competition. Had the competition been the 1964 A-bodies from General Motors—the GTO, Chevelle, Skylark, and F-85 Cutlass—the Charger might have appeared more contemporary. Instead, Chrysler dropped it into a market where it would have to compete with restyled A-bodies from General Motors. Rather than the slab-sided body panels of the original A-cars, the 1966 models featured what was referred to as "Coke-bottle" styling. Cars earned this nickname by having more rounded body panels with arcs over the wheel wells, making them resemble bottles of Coca-Cola laid on their sides.

For 1968, Chrysler applied its interpretation of the Coke-bottle treatment to its struggling B-body cars. The resulting machines, with their smooth lines, subtly rounded curves, and near-perfect proportions, were some of the most stunning automobiles of the classic muscle-car era. Dodge introduced a restyled Charger and Coronet R/T for 1968, along with a new R/T rendition of the Charger. The Charger took the Coke-bottle shape further than any of the other B-body cars; the R/T version differed from the standard Charger primarily in the addition of a few cosmetic badges, though it did include one critically important piece of standard equipment: the 375-horsepower 440. Of course, the Hemi was an option. When Tom McCahill tested a Hemi-powered 1968 Charger R/T for the December 1967 issue of *Mechanix Illustrated*, he described the car as being "as wild as a Killarney bat after a quick dip into a tub of LSD."

Chrysler made some improvements to the street Hemi for 1968. A slightly higher compression ratio (10.3:1) and a revised camshaft (still with solid lifters) bumped torque to 490 pound-feet (though claimed horsepower remained at 425), putting the Hemi back on top of Chrysler's performance ladder. Buyers once again had a reason to dig deep into their wallets to get the Hemi option. Plymouth added a companion model for the GTX, a raw street racer even more bare bones than the R/T. This represented a move in the opposite direction from the trends that muscle cars had been following throughout the decade. They had grown larger, heavier, more luxurious—in other words, flabbier. Plymouth thought there might be a market for a trimmed-down hot rod. It stripped the restyled B-body chassis of all frills, such as bucket seats and carpeting, endowed the car with the heavy-duty suspension from Chrysler's police package, and gave it the 335-horsepower version of the 383 as the base engine. Best of all, they priced the car at $2,896, making it the performance bargain of the classic muscle-car era.

Restraint hadn't been working so well for Chrysler; with the Road Runner, restraint went the way of the push-button transmission. In one of the most outrageous marketing moves of the period, Plymouth licensed the use of the popular Warner Brothers' character and named the car after the cartoon bird. The hot rod Plymouth featured graphics of

This 1971 Hemi Challenger is the most heavily optioned E-body Chrysler ever built. In addition to a sunroof, it had a telephone.

"Mr. Norm" Kraus's Grand Spaulding Dodge shop in Chicago was known nationwide as the best destination in the world for getting a Hemi to run properly.

the Road Runner as well as a dual-toned horn designed to ape the character's distinctive "meep-meep" voice. This was not a machine for the shrinking violet who wanted an inconspicuous car. Best of all, it could be ordered with the improved 426 Hemi. When so equipped, the lightweight Road Runner became the fastest regular production stock car of the 1960s.

Encouraged by Plymouth's success, Dodge developed its own cartoon car midway through the 1968 sales year. Rather than license an existing cartoon character, it created its own: the Super Bee. Like the Road Runner, the Super Bee was a stripped-down version of Dodge's B-body coupe—the Coronet—that came with a standard 383 Magnum engine and a four-speed transmission. And like the Road Runner, the Super Bee could be ordered with an optional 426 Hemi engine.

Most people looking to race a Mopar product in 1968 bought one of the stripped-down B-body cars—the Road Runner or the Super Bee—and ordered the optional Hemi engine. From there, they built their own drag cars using aftermarket parts and/or parts from Chrysler's Mopar parts division. As had been the case in 1966, Chrysler offered no turnkey racing version of the B-body in 1968.

The Hemi-powered B-bodies performed well, but some hardcore racers wanted more. And the factory race development folks had plenty more in the works. Late in 1967 Dick Maxwell, who worked for Bob Cahill in product planning for race development, proposed building the racing department's most radical racing concept yet. On February 20, 1968, they sent a letter to dealers explaining what that concept would be: Hemi engines stuffed into the company's small A-body cars, the Plymouth Barracuda (sales code B029) and the Dodge Dart Super Stock (sales code L023). The engine was basically a bone-stock street Hemi, but when mounted in one of these extremely light cars (3,000 pounds), the result was one of the most potent racing specials built during the classic muscle-car era.

These cars were designed to fall within the rules of all major sanctioning organizations—they would not have, for example, rear axles that were moved forward 15 inches in the chassis. To comply with NHRA regulations, they were given a production code (code 366) and received VINs, meaning they could conceivably be licensed for street use. In order to meet NHRA homologation requirements, which had recently been lowered, Chrysler built seventy Hemi Barracudas and seventy Hemi Darts. These cars started out life on the assembly line at Chrysler's Hamtramck, Michigan, plant, complete with 383-cubic-inch

ABOVE: With the new 1970 E-body models, Chrysler finally had the styling the market wanted—just as the muscle car market was disappearing.

LEFT: In addition to the Hemi engine, this 1970 'Cuda packed virtually every option on Plymouth's order sheet, like rear-window defogger, power windows, and AM/FM stereo radio.

B-block engines but without any carpet or sound insulation, and were shipped to Hurst Performance, where they received their Hemi engines. The cars were then shipped back to a storage facility in Detroit, where most buyers came and picked them up.

The cars those buyers received were body-in-white units still waiting to be painted in the owner's racing livery. The front fenders and hood were made of fiberglass and finished in black gel coat, rather than the gray primer that covered the metal body panels. In order to save weight, there were no hinges on the hood; the entire assembly was held in place by four pins and lifted straight up. (Late in the following year, this same design would see use on the A12 B-body cars.) The doors and front bumper were acid-dipped to further reduce weight.

Testing showed these cars to be capable of breaking into the 10-second quarter-mile bracket, and with a little tweaking they could easily dip down into the 9s. Since they were basically stock production cars, they qualified for a wide variety of different classes, making them very desirable race cars. Chrysler sold every example it built before the last car left Hurst's shop.

FLEXING MOPAR MUSCLE

The E-body convertibles were poor choices for Hemi power and not many people ordered them, but their rarity makes them valuable today.

Sales of the redesigned 1968 Charger exploded to nearly 100,000 units, topping the sales of Pontiac's GTO, which *Motor Trend* magazine had named its car of the year. Nearly 75,000 Charger buyers chose the standard 383-equipped car, and the bulk of the rest selected the 440-equipped R/T. The remaining hardcore types bought the brutal Hemi. Chrysler's other B-bodied muscle cars sold well, too, especially the bare-bones Road Runner. Plymouth moved 44,595 examples of their outrageous cartoon cars for 1968. The Super Bee also sold

well, pushing total sales of B-body muscle cars to 173,872 units. This was on top of the sales of pedestrian B-body Coronets, Belvederes, and Satellites, which totaled 582,315 units. The year was a very good one for Chrysler Corporation.

Perhaps the most remarkable statistic for all of 1968, at least regarding automobile sales, was the doubling of the number of buyers selecting the optional Hemi engine. Chrysler sold 2,276 Hemi-powered B-bodies in 1968, almost half of those being lightweight Road Runners. This may have been due to the fact that the Hemi was the only optional engine for Road Runner buyers wanting to step up from the 383 B-block engine—a 440-cubic-inch RB engine wouldn't become available in this model until late in the following year.

By 1968, the development of normally aspirated pushrod V-8 engines had reached the upper limits of horsepower, at least before the advent of improved electronic engine management technology. This was especially true in NASCAR racing, which had strict rules prohibiting forced induction, multiple carburetion, and fuel injection. Manufacturers wanting to win NASCAR championships had to resort to methods other than increasing raw horsepower to attain a top-speed advantage over the competition. The most promising way to gain extra speed was to improve aerodynamic design—a small increase in aerodynamic efficiency increased top speed as much as a large increase in total horsepower output.

For 1968, Ford introduced a new car that would become the basis for its NASCAR racing effort: the Torino GT. The Torino had an aerodynamic shape that flat-out worked on NASCAR's superspeedways. Driver David Pearson dominated the 1968 season in a Torino

ABOVE: This very car served as the model for the car Don Johnson drove in the television series *Nash Bridges*.

FOLLOWING PAGES: This is the very last Hemi 'Cuda ever built. Period. Originally shipped to France, it is thought to have been purchased by French author Françoise Sagan, who was as famous for her love of fast cars as for her enjoyment of cocaine and morphine.

GT prepared by Holman-Moody, winning sixteen races and finishing in the top five 36 times. The Torino's aerodynamic design had helped Ford break the Hemi's recent dominance of NASCAR's Grand National series.

After getting their corporate butts handed to them in 1968, Chrysler's designers took the aerodynamically awful Dodge Charger into the wind tunnel and began crafting a car as slippery as the Ford Torino and its twin, the Mercury Cyclone. The most notable features of the car that resulted from this work, the Charger 500, were a flush-mounted front grille and a flush-mounted rear window in place of the tunnel-type rear window used on the regular production Charger. Though stylish, this tunnel contributed to terrible airflow over the car and held down top speeds on NASCAR track.

Chrysler took its much-improved aerodynamic package to Daytona for the running of the 1969 Daytona 500. Unfortunately for Chrysler, Ford presented an even more aerodynamic version of the Torino and Cyclone couplet, the Torino Talladega and the Cyclone Spoiler. The Ford cars used the same basic aerodynamic tricks as the Charger 500—flush grille, flush-mounted glass—to greater effect. A Ford Talladega driven by LeeRoy Yarbrough won the 500 that year, and Pearson went on to win his second straight Grand National championship.

At this point Chrysler declared all-out war on Ford, as well as any other company impudent enough to challenge Mopar supremacy on NASCAR's superspeedways. Its designers went back to the wind tunnel and emerged with the single most insane automobile of the entire muscle-car era: the Dodge Daytona. At its front the new Daytona featured an 18-inch prosthetic nose, designed to reduce frontal area and provide downforce at speed. In back, to balance the downforce up front, the car featured a huge wing placed on 23-inch-tall uprights. To provide downforce in racing, the wing needed to be raised only 12 inches from the rear deck, but Dodge designers placed it almost twice that high to allow the trunk lid to open on the street-going versions of the car the company would have to build to homologate the design. This aerodynamic package made the racing version of the car good for top speeds of nearly 250 miles per hour.

Plymouth created its own version of the winged car, the Superbird, later in the year. It used a similar wing and nose but had to improvise a bit on the roof design. Though the stock Road Runner had a more aerodynamically efficient rear window area than the stock Charger, the Charger's tunnel design lent itself to creating a more efficient fastback by simply covering the tunnel with a window. The rear sail area of the Road Runner had to be extended to create as efficient a design. To cover up the cobbled-together bodywork around the rear window, all production Superbirds featured vinyl roof covers.

Unlike the scoop that protruded from the hood of Pontiac's Trans Am solely for decorative effect, the "shaker" hood scoops on Hemi E-bodies were functional.

Both cars were built offsite by a company called Creative Industries, which had to hustle to build enough street-legal cars by the January 1, 1970, deadline to homologate the car for NASCAR racing for that year. The results were worth the effort. The Mopars humiliated Ford on NASCAR tracks, winning thirty-eight of forty-eight Grand National races. They would have won even more had tire technology been up to the speeds produced by the amazing winged cars. Tire failure led to some of the hairiest crashes in NASCAR history, and the combined threat of deadly crashes and total Chrysler domination led Bill France to institute a rule change that would keep the winged cars off of NASCAR tracks following the 1970 season. Beginning in 1971, anything NASCAR determined was a "specialty car" (in other words, any car that Bill France thought was too odd) would have to run with a 305-cubic-inch engine. In one stroke of his pen, France killed off both the winged Chryslers and the aerodynamic Fords. When Chrysler redesigned the B-body lineup for 1971, the winged cars disappeared. Since they would not be competitive in NASCAR racing, there was little point in spending the money to develop winged versions of the new cars.

Engine bays were starting to get cluttered with pollution gear by the early 1970s, spelling doom for the Hemi design.

For 1969, Chrysler chose not to mess with a good thing, leaving its lineup largely unchanged. Likewise, the Hemi engine returned unchanged, at least internally—in keeping with the psychedelic zeitgeist of the time, all Hemi-powered cars now featured a functional hood scoop. Owners opened and closed these cable-operated scoops via push-pull buttons mounted inside the cabs. Dodge called its system Ramcharger, and Plymouth gave its system the catchy name Air Grabber.

Halfway through the model year, the Super Bee and Road Runner models received an engine option that would provide strong competition for the Hemi: the A12. Buyers who ordered the A12 option received a trio of Holley two-barrel carburetors mounted atop a specially designed, Edelbrock-built aluminum intake manifold feeding a high-performance 440-cubic-inch engine. In stock form this engine cranked out 390 horsepower and 490 pound-feet of torque. Because this massive reserve of twisting force was available at much lower engine speeds than was the torque of the Hemi, which had been designed to run up the top of its rev range, a well-tuned A12 car would run away from any stock Hemi at a stoplight. To cope with the added 15 horsepower, the engine received beefier valvetrain components, meaning that the A12 was built almost to the high specifications of the Hemi. Although expensive, at $462.80, the A12 was still less than half of the Hemi's price.

The A12 spelled real trouble for Hemi sales; even the guys at the Woodward Avenue garage were distracted by this new engine package. While Chrysler's NASCAR effort continued to rely on the Hemi, the stock-car program was focused on aerodynamics more

than engine development. The drag-racing program didn't produce any Hemi-powered
specials for 1969, choosing instead to work with the newly reinvigorated RB engine. Hemi
sales fell to 1,362 units for 1969. It seemed that the time for building hairy-chested solid-
lifter race engines for the street was coming to a close.

THIS IS THE END

In 1970 Chrysler continued to develop ultra-high-performance machines, even though the
writing was on the wall for muscle cars. That year went down as the peak for muscle-car
performance; everyone in the industry knew it would be all downhill from there. In 1971, US
automakers began to detune their engines with lower compression ratios, retarded ignition,
milder camshafts, and increasingly restrictive intake and exhaust systems. This was in
preparation for the coming of unleaded, lower-octane gasoline, which the government had
mandated all cars would burn beginning with the 1975 model year.

After July 1, 1974, gas stations would begin phasing out gasoline with tetraethyl lead as
an additive. Lead had been added to gasoline since before World War II to prevent engine
detonation, allowing the use of the higher compression ratios that enabled the Hemi to
produce so much horsepower. But it was a nasty carcinogenic substance that caused birth
defects, developmental disabilities, and all sorts of problems with the environment, though

its role in these problems wasn't clearly understood at the time. What was known was that the Environmental Protection Agency planned to institute emissions requirements beginning in 1975 that would require most automakers to install catalytic converters in their exhaust system. These converters used platinum-coated beads to reduce the toxic emissions in automotive exhaust; lead stuck to the beads and plugged up the exhaust system.

Not only did this curtail the future production of Hemi-powered muscle cars, it spelled trouble for the examples Chrysler had already built. By 1978 it would be virtually impossible to buy pump gas with a high enough octane rating to prevent a high-compression Hemi engine from chewing itself to bits.

As if impending government-mandated strangulation wasn't bad enough, insurance companies were starting to exert a negative influence on muscle-car sales as well. The equation of high-horsepower, low-weight cars plus young drivers yielded the sum of exorbitantly high premiums. While many baby boomers could afford the relatively low prices the manufacturers charged for muscle cars, they were starting to have problems affording the steep costs of insuring the beasts, and the Hemi was the most beastly muscle car of them all. If the high purchase price of the Hemi wasn't deterrent enough for many buyers, the costly insurance would keep all but the most dedicated speed freak from driving a Hemi out of a Dodge or Plymouth dealership.

The future of the muscle car looked bleak, but Chrysler intended to build its powerful street fighters until the federal government pried the last Hemi from its cold, dead corporate fingers, and damn the insurance companies and the EPA.

This is one of just 28 Hemi Road Runners that Chrysler equipped with four-speed transmissions in 1971.

As the 1960s came to a close, Chrysler was still not a player in the lucrative pony-car market, but the company finally had plans to change that situation. To keep development costs down, Chrysler designers took the cowl and other chassis components under development for the next-generation B-body cars and built a pony car around them. Internally coded the "E-body," the car featured the classical proportions that Virgil Exner had admired in the sporty Italian cars of the 1940s and 1950s—long hood, short deck, small passenger compartment. These design features, which exemplified what Exner called the school of "Italian simplicity," had come to define the pony-car genre.

The E-body was actually a pair of cars: the Dodge Challenger and Plymouth Barracuda, introduced for the 1970 model year. The Challenger rode on a wheelbase that was stretched 2 inches over its Plymouth counterpart—112 inches versus 110 inches—and was 4.3 inches longer than the Barracuda overall. Technically, the models broke little new ground, but they did blur the line between pony car and muscle car. Because they used the basic front cowl from the impending B-body redesign, the new E-bodies were larger than their pony-car competitors from Ford and General Motors, but they were smaller than Chrysler's B-body muscle cars.

While it led to a car that was physically larger than the competition, using B-body components allowed Chrysler to offer the E-body with any engine in the company's stable, including the mighty Hemi, which, when mounted in the new E body cars, created the most potent muscle-car package in the Mopar lineup. The sporty version of the 1970 Challenger was the R/T, which featured the 383-cubic-inch B-block engine with Magnum heads as its base engine, though a buyer could choose an optional 440-cubic-inch RB engine with either a single four-barrel or three two-barrel carburetors. If a buyer intended to do some serious racing, he or she ordered a 426 Hemi. The performance version of the Barracuda was simply called the 'Cuda, and it had the same selection of engines.

Because the small-block 340 made for a much better street engine in a convertible 'Cuda, mounting a Hemi between the front wheels took serious commitment.

'Cuda buyers who opted for the Hemi option received a shaker hood-scoop system as standard equipment. (Challenger buyers could order the system as an extra-cost option.) This consisted of a giant intake snorkel over the air cleaner that protruded up through a gaping hole in the hood. The system didn't lend itself to use in inclement weather, and it didn't have much effect on performance one way or the other, but few would argue that it is the single coolest hood scoop produced during the muscle-car era.

In 1970 Chrysler installed a new hydraulic-lifter cam in the Hemi, finally eliminating periodic valve adjustments from the Hemi owner's long list of maintenance chores. Horsepower remained unchanged, at 425, but given the untapped potential of the engine, it was relatively easy for Chrysler engineers to adjust this number up or down as needed. For anyone except a racer who intended to build a 1,000-horsepower drag motor, the hydraulic lifters were a step in the right direction. Valve adjustments were labor-intensive affairs on the big, complex Hemi, and eliminating them made the engine a more viable alternative for many buyers. Or, at least, for rich buyers—ordering a Hemi engine added $871.45 to the $3,164 base price of a 1971 'Cuda, dangerously close to a 30-percent price increase. In contrast, the torque-monster 440 Six-Pack added just $250 to the bottom line.

Chrysler's last big money shot in the muscle-car wars was its redesigned 1971 B-body platform. The new models retained the Coke-bottle styling of the previous generation of cars but adopted long-hood, short-deck pony-car proportions. The company maintained the Charger, Super Bee, Road Runner, and GTX versions of the B-body chassis, but the Coronet R/T didn't make the cut. The killer big-block engines that had earned Mopar its legendary performance reputation all stuck around for 1971, including the Six-Pack version of the 440 and the omnipotent 426 Hemi. Chrysler followed the lead of General Motors and reduced the compression ratio of the RB engine for 1971 but held the line with the Hemi. That engine returned unchanged in 1971, making it the last original muscle-car combatant still doing battle with its horsepower intact.

While the Hemi didn't receive any mechanical changes for 1971, it did have a lower horsepower rating. That was because of a change in the way horsepower would be rated. Previously American automakers rated their engines in terms of SAE (Society of Automotive Engineers) gross horsepower, which was measured using a blueprinted test engine running on a stand without accessories, mufflers, or emissions control devices. This did not provide an accurate measurement of the power output of an engine installed in a street car. Gross horsepower figures were also easily manipulated by carmakers; they could be inflated to make a car appear more muscular or deflated to appease insurance companies or to qualify a car for a certain class of racing.

Beginning in 1972, US carmakers would have to quote power exclusively in SAE net horsepower, which rated the power of the engine with all accessories and standard intake and exhaust systems installed. This provided a more accurate measurement of a given car's true output, but the overall numbers were lower. Chrysler began using the new rating system in 1971, giving both the old SAE gross figures and the new SAE net figures. While the old SAE gross rating remained the same for the Hemi (425 horsepower, 490 pound-feet of torque), the new net rating was 350 horsepower at 5,000 rpm, and the SAE net torque rating fell to 390 pound-feet at 5,000 rpm.

This was a time before online communities debated such subjects. It was before the Internet, even before cable television, and genuine information was hard to come by. Most hot rodders operated in a fog of misinformation and old wives' tales. People believed the power ratings printed in advertising brochures because often this was the only information available regarding power output. The average buyer didn't know SAE gross from SAE net; a person only knew that a Hemi with 425 horsepower was better than a Hemi with 350 horsepower.

In 1972 Chrysler further detuned its engines in preparation for the impending switch to low-octane unleaded fuel. The B-body cars could still be ordered with big-block engines, but these engines struggled to put out as much power as the small-blocks of a few years earlier. The 340-cubic-inch engine was the top offering in the E-body cars for 1972; the big-block engine had disappeared from their option lists.

And to no one's surprise, the Hemi had finally become extinct. Redesigning this gas-guzzling dinosaur—which was both low volume (Chrysler built just 486 Hemi engines in 1971) and labor intensive (each engine was still practically hand-assembled)—to meet upcoming emissions regulations and run on the swill that would soon pass for pump gas would have been astronomically expensive. Like all the other US automakers of the time, Chrysler was expending every available resource in order to redesign its passenger-car engines for the coming changes mandated by the government; there was simply no money available to nurse the Hemi into this brave, new world. Tom Hoover and the rest of the hot rodders at Chrysler made a valiant attempt to bring their beloved Hemi into the coming dark ages of performance cars, but the forces allied against them were unbeatable.

This shortage of funds impacted every facet of Chrysler Corporation, including its racing program, which was radically curtailed for 1971. That year Chrysler sponsored only two race teams in NASCAR (which began running Winston Cup races in 1971). Richard Petty would go on to win a few more championships, but his last title in a Chrysler product came in 1975, forever ending Chrysler's domination of the series.

Support money for drag racing also dried up. Dodges and Plymouths ruled the Pro Stock and Super Stock classes, and there was little need to waste limited resources to humiliate the competition even further. Tom Hoover and his crew continued to develop the Hemi for top racers such as Ronnie Sox and Dick Landy, but there would be no more production runs of specialized drag-racing cars. Without the excuse of building Hemi cars to support racing activities, and with the sales of street Hemis so low as to be almost immeasurable, further Hemi production was unjustifiable. Almost before anyone realized what was happening, the Hemi had disappeared, and one of the most exciting periods in automotive history had come to an end.

Even though making any sort of legitimate business case for the Hemi would have been impossible, the engineering types at Chrysler loved their big elephant engine and would make heroic efforts to keep it alive into the 1970s. They even developed the A279 Hemi, a completely new engine originally intended for introduction in the 1972 model year.

This engine, known internally as the ball-stud Hemi, would have maintained a high level of performance while still complying with the upcoming emissions standards. It would have had the added benefit of being much cheaper to produce than the 426, which appealed to Chrysler's bean counters; it would have even been cheaper to produce than the wedge engines. Cost savings would come from a new, less-complicated valve operating system that used ball studs at each stamped-metal rocker arm, much like the system used in General Motors engines, instead of the forged rocker arm and shaft system that Chrysler had always used in its high-performance engines.

If all had gone according to plan, the engine would have been built in both 400-cubic-inch and 440-cubic-inch forms, with the performance of the 440 version falling midway between the Hemi and the four-barrel version of the RB engine. Chrysler engineers got as far as testing prototype ball-stud Hemis, but in the end Chrysler decided to pass on the A279 design. The future of high-performance cars was looking grim by 1972.

THE KEITH BLACK 426

Even though Chrysler stopped building the street Hemi after 1971, the engine's phenomenal success at the drag strip meant that a small specialty market would continue to need it. Ed Donovan had already begun to fulfill the demands of that market even before the original street Hemi went out of production. In 1957, Donovan, a drag racer who had cut his teeth in the aftermarket industry working at Offenhauser, started Donovan Engineering, a manufacturer of aftermarket speed equipment focusing on the needs of drag racing. Donovan was a big fan of the 392 Hemi, and his ultimate ambition was to build and market an aluminum block based on that engine, only without the early Hemi's flaws. With all the aftermarket speed equipment available for the early Hemi at the time, a racer could buy Donovan's block and build a competitive racing engine.

Donovan completed the developmental work in 1970 and began production of his aluminum Hemi engine block. To ensure that all equipment designed for the factory block would bolt right on to his block, he retained all the major dimensions of the original. His only change was giving the cylinders a 0.125-inch overbore, so his engine displaced 417 cubic inches.

Most aluminum racing blocks at the time were solid aluminum with pressed-in steel cylinder liners. All internal passages were milled into the aluminum. Donovan used an open-cast design with chrome-moly wet-sleeve liners. This design weighed less than 200 pounds and had the added advantage of allowing easy replacement of the cylinder liners. It was also strong enough to handle much more power than the original factory block

ABOVE AND OPPOSITE: **Ed Pink built the engine for Kenny Bernstein's 1980 *Arrow* Funny Car using a Keith Black Hemi block and heads.**

could handle. To further strengthen the engine, Donovan increased the size of the main bearing supports, addressing a problem that Chrysler had solved with the B-block engines.

Donovan began selling his 417 Hemi to drag racers in 1971. Top Fuel racer John Wiebe raced one for the very first time at the NHRA Supernationals in Ontario, California, setting the low time of 6.53 seconds for that year's Supernationals. Wiebe was the top qualifier and finished the event in the runner-up position. By 1972 it seemed every other dragster was running a Donovan 417 Hemi, and Donovan counted drag-racing royalty such as Big Daddy Garlits among his satisfied customers. Donovan Engineering grew into an engine-building empire, and the firm continues to build the 417 Hemi to this day. Ed Donovan, who died of cancer in 1989, was posthumously inducted into the Motorsports Hall of Fame in 2003.

Keith Black was one of the people getting beaten by Donovan and his 417 Hemis. Black became involved with the hot-rod culture flourishing in his native Southern California when he was still in high school. A naturally gifted mechanic, he began to work on the engines of the drag boats that raced in California's Salton Sea. He started out small, fixing a part here and there, but as more people became familiar with his remarkable skills, he began to get more work, and his hobby turned into a career.

Early on he worked on a few Oldsmobile and Cadillac engines, since those were the first OHV V-8 engines available. When Chrysler introduced the Hemi, however, he focused on that powerplant because he believed it had more potential as a race engine. In 1959 he started Keith Black Race Engines. The drag-racing community took note of his successful boat-racing engines, and soon he was building race motors for some of the top drivers, including Don Prudhomme. When the Donovan 417 hit the scene, Black found himself losing business because people were racing Donovan's new aluminum engine instead of the factory cast-iron 426 engines Black was building. To make matters worse, Chrysler was stopping production of the 426 Hemi.

Black had already approached Chrysler with a proposal to build an aluminum-block 426 but hadn't been able to generate any traction with that idea. When the aluminum Donovan 417 came on the scene and started beating the cast-iron Chrysler Hemis, Bob Cahill and the other folks remaining at Chrysler's racing department weren't pleased. They decided to help Black with his project, provided it didn't cost Chrysler any money; by then Chrysler's racing budget was so low as to almost be a negative number. Still, they were able to send Black the latest engineering drawings for the Hemi so he had all the proper dimensions to work with.

It took Black a couple of years to develop the engine and find quality vendors to produce it, but he introduced his aluminum version of Chrysler's 426 Hemi in 1974. It became the industry standard—between 1975 and 1984, cars powered by Keith Black's aluminum engine blocks held every Top Fuel record. The production Hemi had passed from the passenger scene, at least for a generation or two, but Black ensured that it would remain the dominant force on America's drag strips.

OPPOSITE: What would this book be without the obligatory photo of a Hemi 'Cuda doing a burnout?

Twenty-First-Century Hemi Muscle

For more than thirty years after the demise of the 426, the Hemi existed only as a low-volume race engine built by specialized aftermarket manufacturers such as Donovan Engineering and Keith Black Race Engines. Meanwhile Hemi-powered cars skyrocketed in value. The mythological engine had earned concrete exchange value.

Chrysler engineers never let go of the idea of a Hemi; it was the Hemi, after all, that had given the company its reputation for engineering excellence. If the engine had become a mythic creature in the world at large, it had attained an almost godlike status within the halls of Chrysler Corporation. Generation after generation of young engineers aspired to follow in the footsteps of the legendary men behind the Hemi—folks like Tom Hoover, Ev Moeller, and Bob Cahill. Their successors were itching to build a new Hemi, and they were about to get their shot at it, thanks to a need for a new truck engine.

OPPOSITE: With 707 horsepower, the Dodge Challenger SRT Hellcat was the most powerful muscle car released up to that point. This 2016 example resides in the Brothers Collection.

By the mid-1990s, the 360-cubic-inch LA-block engine powering Dodge pickup trucks needed to be replaced. After all, the basic design of the engine dated back to the poly V-8s of the 1950s. The trucks needed an engine that was both powerful and efficient, one that would meet upcoming emissions standards for years to come. Rich Schaum proposed building a new V-8 in 1996, and Robert Lee, who was in charge of engine development, organized a team to begin development work.

Lee's team studied every engine system on the market—overhead cams, four-valves-per cylinder heads, alternative combustion-chamber designs—and discovered that the flat six in Porsche's then-new Boxster was one of the most efficient engines being built. The Boxster featured domed combustion chambers. Lee and his crew looked further into the benefits of a hemi head, and the more they looked, the more benefits they found. What was a good idea in the 1940s remained a good idea in the 1990s.

Lee locked his team away in Chrysler's technical center in Auburn Hills, Michigan, to explore this concept further. They worked to develop a hemispherical combustion-chamber design that was as efficient at reducing emissions as it was at producing power. The engine they came up with featured an iron block with aluminum cylinder heads. The cylinders had but two valves apiece, making this a true hemi rather than a pent-roof design like the four-valve Porsche engine. Unlike the Hemis of old, the new version was a longer-stroke design, though it was still slightly oversquare, with bore and stroke measuring 3.9 inches and 3.6 inches, respectively, for a total displacement of 5.7 liters (or 345 cubic inches, in muscle-car language). In base form, it put out 340 horsepower and 387 pound-feet of torque. The main bearing caps were held in place by two vertical bolts, along with a pair of cross bolts.

Lee's team managed to keep the new Hemi's existence a secret until it was just about to be made public. To help keep the project from being exposed, they never referred to it as a "hemi," even though the engine used hemispherical combustion chambers.

Although this was to ensure secrecy, part of the reason the new engine was not called a Hemi stemmed from respect for the Hemi name within Chrysler. By this time the Hemi had become acknowledged as the single greatest engineering accomplishment of any American auto manufacturer during the classic muscle-car era, and you did not take the name Hemi in vain at Chrysler. If Lee and his engineers were going to use the moniker, the engine they produced had to be damned good. They wouldn't call it a Hemi until it had proved its worth. It did. The engine handled every durability torture test to which the team subjected it.

THAT THING GOT A HEMI?

The engine originally debuted in the 2003 model year pickups. Since the engine had proven itself worthy of the name Hemi, Chrysler's marketing folks made good use of it, plastering it all over the new trucks. They even made it the central component of a wildly successful

RIGHT: The hottest new muscle car from Chrysler in the new millennium was the SRT-8 version of the 300.

BELOW: Buyers could also get their muscle car in station wagon form with the SRT-8 version of the Dodge Magnum.

advertising campaign. The ad consisted of a couple of losers in a rust-bucket car pulling up to the new Dodge pickup and asking the pickup driver, "That thing got a Hemi?" Of course it did, and of course the pickup driver exited the scene in a blaze of burnt rubber. When he was gone, the dillweed in the rust bucket had only one thing to say: "Sweet."

The ad told the world that Chrysler fully recognized the iconic status that its Hemi engine had achieved. And it made clear that the company (which was then part of DaimlerChrysler) knew how to market that icon to maximum effect. The next step in marketing the Hemi, however, would have to involve mounting it in something sportier than a truck. Pickups are the most important source of revenue for any US automaker, but they aren't muscle cars, so for 2004 Chrysler introduced a brand-new 300C. The company had revived the 300 nameplate several years earlier, but the car to which it was attached—the 300M—had been a milquetoast front-wheel-drive sedan. The completely new 300C was a fire-breathing, rear-wheel-drive, muscular machine, thanks to its Hemi engine.

The 300C was a great car, but muscular or not, it was a luxury sedan and not a muscle car, so Dodge revived the Charger name for the 2006 model year. In Daytona R/T form, the car was powered by a 350-horsepower Hemi. This 345-cubic-inch pushrod V-8 matched its fabled 426-cubic-inch predecessor's SAE net horsepower rating as well as the 390 pound-feet of torque (SAE net) that the older 426-cubic-inch version produced. And it did all this while still earning an EPA-estimated 25 miles per gallon, about five times as the fuel efficiency of its legendary forebear.

For 2006 Chrysler brought back the Charger as a four-door muscle car.

Chrysler marketed the new Charger to law enforcement agencies, releasing endorphins in police brains across the United States.

Chrysler's old racing department never really went away. Even in the darkest days of the 1970s and early 1980s smog-motor era, a time when Chrysler Corporation was seeking government help to stay afloat, speed-crazed miscreants within the company could be found in dark corners, plotting high-performance mischief. Such clandestine development led to cars such as the Viper and the Prowler. The acronym for this group morphed over the years, going from Specialty Vehicle Engineering (SVE) to Performance Vehicle Operations (PVO) to Street & Racing Technology (SRT). But whatever letters they used, these people have always been the spiritual descendants of the hot-rod boys and Ram Chargers who used to tear up Woodward Avenue back in the day. As could be expected, this group had its collective way with the new Hemi.

The coupling of the SRT division with the new Hemi engine resulted in the SRT8, a Hemi that produced 425 horsepower and 420 pound-feet of torque. This modern Hemi produced net ratings that equaled the old engine's gross ratings. That was enough to propel the Charger through the quarter mile in the 13-second bracket, despite the car's weighing a hefty 4,200 pounds.

The SRT8 got its extra horsepower honestly, through more cubic inches—the SRT8 displacement grew to 370 cubic inches (or 6.1 liters). The increased displacement came via a bore increased to 4.05 inches. The cylinder block had a reinforced bulkhead to handle the extra loads generated by the larger pistons. The engine used a relatively high compression ratio (10.3:1), and jets squirted oil at the underside of the pistons to help keep them cool. Like its predecessor, the 426 street Hemi, the SRT8 was loaded with high-grade performance parts. It had a billet-steel camshaft with more lift, longer duration, and more overlap than the cam in the smaller engine. Hollow stemmed intake valves measured 2.07 inches, versus 2 inches for the 345-cubic-inch engine, and the 1.59-inch exhaust valves were sodium filled. Fuel entered the engine via a freer-flowing fuel-injection system, and spent gases exited via genuine tubular headers.

And like its predecessor, the new top-dog Hemi engine was expensive. All those good parts didn't come cheap, whether they made up an old street Hemi or the

BELOW AND FOLLOWING PAGES: The 2006 Dodge Challenger concept car lit the automotive world on fire, looking like a Challenger from the 1970s that had developed a paunch . . . much like its target audience.

twenty-first-century engine. The 2006 Charger Daytona R/T cost $35,794. The 2006 Charger SRT8 cost $43,730 (though, in all fairness, the SRT8 price included a $2,100 gas-guzzler tax).

REBIRTH OF THE CHALLENGER

Everyone expected Dodge to bring back the Charger. What no one expected was that the new car would have four doors—in the past, all muscle cars had two doors.

For those who refused to accept a four-door muscle car, DaimlerChrysler developed a modern rendition of Dodge's original pony car, the Challenger. (There would be no new 'Cuda, since DaimlerChrysler—the temporary and unhappy company that formed when Daimler-Benz bought Chrysler in the 1990s and dissolved when Daimler sold Chrysler to the investment group Cerberus Capital Management in 2007—had pulled the plug on the Plymouth brand after the 2001 model year.)

The new Challenger was larger than its illustrious ancestor. Its 116-inch wheelbase was 6 inches longer than that of the original 1970 E-body Challenger (8 inches longer than Plymouth's Barracuda), and its overall length of 197.8 inches was almost 9 inches longer than the original car (over 11 inches longer than the original 'Cuda). Despite these larger proportions, Dodge designers did a commendable job re-creating the classic E-body look in a car with modern aerodynamic efficiency. Perhaps the most visible differences were the shorter front and rear overhangs on the new car.

One area where the new Challenger paid faithful tribute to the original was in its engine bay. Therein resided an SRT8 Hemi, at least on the first batch of cars produced in early 2008. The new Challenger would turn in 13-second-flat quarter-mile times and hit a top speed of 174 miles per hour.

Chrysler introduced this car at the January 2006 North American International Auto Show in Detroit, to universally positive response. In August of that year, the company announced it would build production versions. SRT8 examples begin rolling off the assembly line in early 2008, all equipped with five-speed automatic transmissions, and production of standard 5.7-liter versions began for the 2009 model year. For 2009 Chrysler offered a six-speed

OPPOSITE: Dodge kicked off the new Challenger era with the 2008 SRT-8, which generated 425 horsepower net versus the previous Hemi's 425 gross horsepower rating.

ABOVE: Dodge followed the 2008 SRT-8 version of the Challenger with the R/T in 2009. While the R/T had a smaller engine producing less horsepower, it marked the debut of a six-speed manual transmission

LEFT: The R/T Challenger's Hemi developed 372 horsepower and 398 lb-ft of torque when coupled to a five-speed automatic, and 375 horsepower when mated to a six-speed manual transmission.

manual transmission with a classic Hurst-style pistol-grip shifter, a design that had become a hallmark of Chrysler muscle cars of the early 1970s. The company capped total production at 6,700 SRT8 units for 2008. This relatively low production volume led to price inflation by dealers, who charged premiums of up to 100 percent over the car's $37,995 base price for the first limited run of SRT8 Challengers.

The first Challenger SRT8—serial number 1—was auctioned off at the Barrett-Jackson Collector Car Auction for $400,000 on January 18, 2008, several weeks before the February 6, 2008, public unveiling of the production car at the Chicago Auto Show. Another Challenger SRT8 bearing the serial number 43—Richard Petty's racing number—was auctioned on eBay on February 13, 2008, as part of the celebration of Petty Enterprises' fiftieth anniversary. As could be expected, that car was painted B5 Blue, otherwise known as "Petty Blue." Chrysler donated proceeds from both auctions to charity.

FIX IT AGAIN, TONY

A funny thing happened on the way to bringing the Challenger into full production: the economy imploded, the banking system collapsed, and Chrysler finally went bankrupt, after skating on the edge of insolvency for much of its first ninety years. In 2009 it finally skated over that edge. It wasn't alone; General Motors filed bankruptcy that year, and both companies went into government receivership.

ABOVE: Chrysler built between 90 and 100 "Drag Pak" Challengers in 2009 to compete in NHRA racing.

RIGHT: The actual output of the Drag Pak engine was never released, but given that the cars could run the quarter mile in fewer than 10 seconds, the estimate of "well over the SRT-8's 425 horsepower" seems a reasonable guess.

This happened during the most tumultuous time in economic history since the Great Depression. Deregulation of the banking industry, particularly the repeal of the Depression-era Glass-Steagall rule in 1999, had turned the Wall Street banks into the world's highest-rolling gambling casinos, and when that house of cards collapsed in the fall of 2008, it took the entire economy with it. The auto industry was especially hard hit. The new Obama administration took over General Motors and more or less nursed it back to health. With Chrysler, the solution was a bit more draconian; the government basically gave it to the Italian automaker Fiat. By 2011 Fiat owned Chrysler outright.

Like Chrysler, Fiat had spent much of its first century dancing with financial ruin, and it wasn't a company with a history of building brutish muscle cars. But it did understand the panache the Hemi engine carried in the muscle-car market. Fiat put very little effort into further development of the 300 and Charger models but did put some muscle into developing performance variants of the Challenger.

Buyers who liked the looks of the car but had no interest in real muscle could order a base-model Challenger SE powered by a V-6 engine, but muscle-car fans stepped up to the R/T version, powered by a version of the 5.7 Hemi. In the Challenger, the Hemi developed 372 horsepower and 398 pound-feet of torque when coupled to a five-speed automatic, and 375 horsepower and pound-feet of torque when mated to a Tremec six-speed manual transmission, which was also available on the SRT8 for the 2009 model

Chrysler borrowed the hood scoop from the Challenger T/A and the striping from the AAR 'Cuda to create its 2010 SEMA Challenger show car.

year. R/T buyers who wanted more performance could order the Track Pak, which included the manual transmission, a limited-slip differential, and self-leveling rear shock absorbers.

For 2010, Dodge offered the Mopar '10 Challenger RT, a limited-production version with special paint, an actual Hurst aftermarket pistol-grip shifter, custom badging, Mopar cold-air intake (which produced a 10-horsepower increase), and a Katzkin-sourced aftermarket interior. Five hundred of the cars were completed at the Mopar Upfit Center in Windsor, Ontario, for the US market, and another 100 were built for the Canadian market.

For 2009 Chrysler began offering the Drag Race Package version of the Challenger to compete in NHRA drag racing. Based on the Dodge SRT8, the Drag Racing Package cars weighed 1,000 pounds less than the street-legal versions thanks to the elimination of everything not needed to blast through the quarter mile as quickly as possible. They also made liberal use of composite, polycarbonate, and lightweight components. The engine was repositioned to improve driveline angle and weight distribution, and the wheelbase was shortened by half an inch. The cars also featured a front cradle with bolt-in crossmember, solid engine mounts, and a solid rear axle rather than the independent rear suspension found on the street versions. Chrysler had to build at least fifty to meet NHRA homologation requirements. The exact number produced isn't known, but it's thought to be between ninety and one hundred. Buyers could choose between engines and transmissions. The cars were capable of sub-10-second quarter-mile times and were competitive in the NHRA A/SA class. Don Garlits bought the very first Challenger "Drag Pak" car and raced it in the NHRA.

For the 2011 model year, Challengers received two new engines, a Pentastar V-6 that few muscle-car fans cared about and a Hemi with the historic displacement of 392 cubic inches. Or so the advertising said; in reality the engine displaced just 391 cubic inches, but the marketing copy seemed more impressive if the copywriters fudged that number by a single cubic inch to give it the same displacement as the final version of the original Hemi. This 6.4-liter Hemi, used in the SRT8 version of the Challenger, produced 470 horsepower and 470 pound-feet of torque. Dodge engineers claimed to have sacrificed peak horsepower ratings for increased low-end torque, and given that the 392 produced 90 pound-feet more torque than the 6.1-liter Hemi at a mere 2,900 rpm, there seems little reason to doubt them. Two transmissions were offered: a five-speed automatic and a six-speed manual. With the 392 Hemi, *Car and Driver* recorded a quarter-mile time of 12.9 seconds at 114 miles per hour.

HELLCAT AND DEMON

For the 2015 model year, Chrysler retired the SRT8 version and replaced it with two models, the SRT 392 and the SRT Hellcat. For 2015, all V-8 Challengers equipped with automatic transmissions received an eight-speed ZF transmission in place of the five-speed unit used in earlier versions. Output of the 6.4-liter Hemi engine in the SRT 392 grew

to 485 horsepower, 15 horsepower more than the previous version, and 475 pound-feet of torque, an increase of 5 pound-feet. Both versions received new Brembo brakes, six-piston units up front and four-piston units in the back.

The Hellcat version received a whole heap more horsepower thanks to a new supercharged 6.2-liter Hemi, rated at 707 horsepower and 650 pound-feet of torque. This engine was also offered in the SRT Hellcat version of the Dodge Charger as well as in the Trackhawk version of Jeep's Grand Cherokee SUV. The Hellcat engine was also sold separately for owners of other Hemi-powered Chrysler products who had the gumption to swap engines. In a nod to the earliest Hemi race cars offered by Chrysler in the 1960s, the

ABOVE AND PREVIOUS PAGES: Wild as it was, the Hellcat was at least built for the street. Future Challengers, not so much.

inner driving light on the left front of the Challenger's grille was removed and replaced with an intake snorkel to funnel air into the engine. The wheel wells were enlarged to accommodate the 20-inch aluminum wheels. When equipped with street-legal drag tires (called "cheater slicks" back in the day), the Hellcat produced quarter-mile times of 10.85 seconds; when equipped with more sensible tires, it ran through the quarter mile in 11.2 seconds at 125 miles per hour. Top speed was right around the 200-mile-per-hour mark.

For 2017 Dodge reintroduced the T/A version of the Challenger with a 5.7-liter Hemi and a T/A 392 with a 6.4-liter Hemi. Both versions featured styling cues from the original T/A (which had an LA small-block V-8 rather than a Hemi), including black painted hoods with center air intakes, black roofs, black deck lids, bodyside graphics, the Challenger SRT Hellcat cold-air induction system, retro houndstooth cloth seats, and white-faced gauges. T/A 392 models added the more powerful 6.4-liter Hemi, Brembo brakes, and 20-inch rims.

For 2018 Dodge introduced the wildest Challenger yet, the SRT Demon, a wide-body version of the Challenger. Like the Hellcat, the Demon used a supercharged 6.2-liter V-8 Hemi, though Chrysler claimed this was an all-new engine. It used a 2.7-liter supercharger to generate 808 horsepower with 91-octane gasoline and 840 horsepower with 100-octane fuel or higher. The Demon produced 770 pound-feet of torque on 100-octane fuel. At 4,254 pounds, the car weighed 215 pounds less than the Hellcat. To handle all that power, it used street-legal drag-racing NT05Rs from Nitto Tire, making the Demon the first production car to come equipped with road-legal radial drag-racing tires. To emphasize how serious a drag-racing tool the Challenger SRT Demon really was, it was also the first production car to feature a drag-racing transmission braking system that Dodge called the "TransBrake," which simultaneously put the transmission in first gear and reverse, holding the Demon stationary while revving the engine to launch at the drag strip.

Buyers also received something called the Demon Crate, which consisted of different electronics, a low-restriction air

The AAR-style hood scoop alone wasn't enough to feed air to the Hellcat's supercharger, so Dodge removed the inboard headlights and mounted additional intake snorkels in their place.

filter, a switch allowing the use of high-octane racing fuel, serialized carbon-fiber instrument panel badges, a kit containing tools with Demon logos, and the Demon Trak Pak. Basically, the Demon Crate contained everything a buyer needed to go drag racing, including skinny front tires and all the tools necessary to put them on after arriving at the track. All of this combined to send the SRT Demon through the quarter mile in just 9.65 seconds at 140.09 miles per hour, making it the quickest production car ever built. It was also the first production car capable of doing a wheelie off the line. Not that anyone could race the SRT Demon in the NHRA; it lacked an NHRA-certified roll cage, which is required if a car's quarter-mile time is under 10 seconds. Because of this, the NHRA banned the Demon from competition. Even so, Dodge sold 3,300 Demons, which started at $84,000, though few buyers were lucky enough to get one at the suggested retail price.

The base 2017 Challenger T/A featured a 5.7-liter Hemi and the 392 T/A featured a 6.4-liter version.

"426 CUBIC INCHES OF LEASHED FURY"

As good as the new cars are, something keeps drawing us back to the old Hemis. It's something less concrete than noise levels and reliability stats. In *Muscle Car Confidential* the late Joe Oldham describes the visceral appeal of the 426 Hemi:

> **As far as ambiance from the driver's seat, no amount of modern technology can match the sheer thrill of being the master of 426 cubic inches of leashed fury . . . There's no real way to describe in words the sound of eight Carter AFB barrels opening up on top of a 426-cubic-inch hemispherical combustion chamber engine. But I'll try. It starts as a low moan, slowly rising into a wail that eventually turns into a shriek, a shriek that threatens to suck not only the surrounding air but also the hood itself and the closest two fenders directly into the shaker hood scoop.**

As was usually the case, Mr. Oldham got right to the very core of the matter. All the aspects of the Hemi's amazing history help account for its mythological status: its racing provenance, its exclusivity, its rarity. But the Hemi experience—that sound, that feel, that brutal *presence*—is the reason the myth of the Hemi lives on stronger than ever.

With the Demon, Dodge took the Challenger to new extremes. This was the most potent Mopar muscle car ever released. The giant hood scoop was needed to feed air to the 2.7-liter supercharger that helped the Demon develop its 840 horsepower.

PHOTOGRAPHY CREDITS

a=all; b=bottom; t=top

Alamy Stock Photos: 26t (David Chapman/Vantage). *Chrysler:* 21, 23, 38, 39, 41, 42, 66, 67, 68–69, 86, 110, 166. *Creative Commons:* 170 (Credit: GPDII). *Getty Images:* 9 (ISC Images & Archives), 32 (ISC Images & Archives), 58–59 (ISC Images & Archives), 101 (ISC Images). *David Gooley:* 133. *Peter Harholdt:* Front cover. *Ron Kimball/KimballStock:* 24–25, 177, 186. *Randy Leffingwell:* 2–3, 4–5, 90, 91, 92–93, 141, 143, 144, 150–151, 155. *Tom Loeser:* 88–89a, 94, 114–115, 118–119, 120a, 122, 123, 126–127, 128, 146, 147b, 148, 152, 153, 156–157, 164–165, 180–181. *Motorbooks Collection:* 11t, 26b, 27, 29, 30, 31a, 33a, 34a, 45b, 57t, 65, 72–73, 113. *David Newhardt:* 6–7, 8, 10a, 13a, 14–15, 17, 18–19, 20, 28a, 35, 36–37, 46, 54–55a, 60, 71, 74, 75, 76–77, 78, 79, 80–81, 82–83, 84–85, 87a, 97, 102, 105, 106, 107, 108, 109, 111, 116, 124, 125, 129a, 130–131, 132, 134, 135, 136–137, 138, 139, 142, 145, 147t, 149, 154, 158, 160, 161, 163, 167a, 168a, 169, 171, 172–173, 174, 175a, 176, 178a, 179, 183, 184–185, 187. *Revs Institute:* 11b (Tom Burnside), 45t (Smith Hempstone Oliver), 49 (George Phillips), 50–51 (George Phillips), 57b (Tom Burnside). *Martyn L. Schorr/DAY ONE:* 95, 98–99, 117, 121, 140, *US Air Force:* 12. *Shutterstock:* endpapers. *Larry Zappone:* 52–53, 62, 63, 64.

INDEX

23 22 21 20 19   1 2 3 4 5

ISBN: 978-0-7603-6519-9

Digital edition published in 2019

eISBN: 978-0-7603-6520-5

Library of Congress Cataloging-in-Publication Data

Names: Holmstrom, Darwin, author.
Title: Hemi muscle : 70 years of Chrysler, Dodge and Plymouth high
  performance / by Darwin Holmstrom.
Description: Beverly, MA : Motorbooks, an imprint of The Quarto Group, 2019.
  | Includes index. |
Identifiers: LCCN 2019017898 (print) | LCCN 2019020623 (ebook) | ISBN
  9780760365205 (E-Book) | ISBN 9780760365199 (hardcover) | ISBN
  9780760365205 (ebook)
Subjects: LCSH: Chrysler automobile--History. | Chrysler
  automobile--Motors--History. | Muscle cars--United States--History. |
  Automobiles--Performance.
Classification: LCC TL215.C55 (ebook) | LCC TL215.C55 H5948 2019 (print) |
  DDC 629.2220973--dc23
LC record available at https://lccn.loc.gov/2019017898

Acquisitions Editor: Zack Miller
Art Director: Cindy Samargia Laun
Cover and Interior Design: Silverglass

Front Cover Image: Peter Harholdt
Back Cover Image: Tom Loeser

Printed in China